Editorial Project Manager
Paul Gardner

Editor in Chief
Sharon Coan, M.S. Ed.

Illustrator
Howard Chaney

Cover Artist
Susan Williams

Art Coordinator
Cheri Macoubrie Wilson

Creative Director
Elayne Roberts

Imaging
Ralph Olmedo, Jr.

Product Manager
Phil Garcia

Trademarks
Trademarked names and graphics appear throughout this book. Instead of listing every firm and entity which owns the trademarks or inserting a trademark symbol with each mention of a trademarked name, the publisher avers that it is using the names and graphics only for editorial purposes and to the benefit of the trademarked owner with no intention of infringing upon that trademark.

Publishers
Rachelle Cracchiolo, M.S. Ed.
Mary Dupuy Smith, M.S. Ed.

INTEGRATING TECHNOLOGY INTO THE LANGUAGE ARTS CURRICULUM

INTERMEDIATE

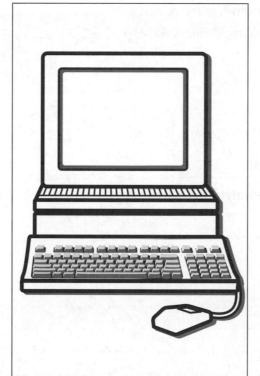

Author

Tracee Sudyka, M.A.

Teacher Created Materials, Inc.
6421 Industry Way
Westminster, CA 92683
www.teachercreated.com

ISBN-1-57690-422-9

©1999 Teacher Created Materials, Inc.
Reprinted, 1999
Made in U.S.A.

TABLE OF CONTENTS

Introduction

    About this Book 4

    How to Use this Book 5

Equipment

    Hardware 6

Management

    Lab Management 10

    Language Arts Classroom Centers 12

    Language Arts Classroom Centers Chart 13

    Diagram of Language Arts Centers Set-Up 14

Assessment

    Performance-Based 15

    Self-Assessment 16

    Self-Assessment Job Performance Record 17

General Software Suggestions 18

The Internet in the Intermediate Classroom 20

Lesson Plans

   Reading

    Internet Library 22

    Book Review Posters 24

    Book Report Slide Shows 27

    Fact Book Research 31

    Story Pyramid 33

    Telecommunications Writing Exchange 35

    Author Research 37

    Candy Production Flow Chart 38

    Stop Action Story Animation 39

    Group Claymation and Animation Comprehension Check 40

    Story Menus 41

    Endangered Animal Research 44

TABLE OF CONTENTS *(cont.)*

Writing

Endangered Animal Research Multimedia Report 46

Keypals 49

Collaborative Stories 50

Personal Newspaper 51

Fairy Tale Slide Shows 54

Laserdisc Descriptive Writing 60

Poetry Anthologies 62

"Choose Your Own Ending" Adventure Story 65

Imagination Express Stories 72

"I Am" Video Poetry 75

Video Stories 77

Speaking

Voice Overs 83

Storytelling 84

Renga Chain Poems 86

Public Service Announcements 88

Newscasts 89

Listening

Vocabulary Videos 92

Vocabulary Bank 94

Pre-Writing Listening Lesson 95

Mystery Picture 96

Monthly Theme Ideas

January: Winter Stories and Scenes 100

February: Black History Reports 102

March: Women in History Biographies 104

April: Earth Day Messages 106

May: Haiku Poetry 108

June: Autobiographies 110

July: My Favorite 112

August: Ocean Life Reports 114

September: Summer Postcards 116

October: Spider Reports 118

November: Native American Reports 120

December: Family Heritage Electronic Cookbook 121

Tips 123

Resources 135

ABOUT THIS BOOK

This book is one in a series of twelve on Integrating Technology into the Curriculum. There are four books—Language Arts, Math, Science, History—on each of three levels (Primary, Intermediate, Challenging). Each book contains management ideas and lesson plans to help you integrate technology into your curriculum.

This book contains ideas and lesson plans that use technology to assist the teacher with meeting Language Arts learning standards. The ideas and lessons in this book are ultimately meant to help the students to:

1. Demonstrate competence in the general skills and strategies of the writing process.

2. Demonstrate competence in the stylistic and rhetorical aspects of writing.

3. Write with a command of the grammatical and mechanical conventions of composition.

4. Effectively gather and use information for research purposes.

5. Demonstrate competence in the general skills and strategies of the reading process.

6. Demonstrate competence in general skills and strategies for reading literature.

7. Demonstrate competence in the general skills and strategies for reading information.

8. Demonstrate competence in applying the reading process to specific types of literary texts.

9. Demonstrate competence in applying the reading process to specific types of informational texts.

10. Demonstrate competence in using different information sources, including those of a technical nature, to accomplish specific tasks.

11. Demonstrate competence in speaking and listening as tools for learning.

12. Demonstrate an understanding of the nature and function of the English language.

13. Demonstrate a familiarity with selected literary works of enduring quality.

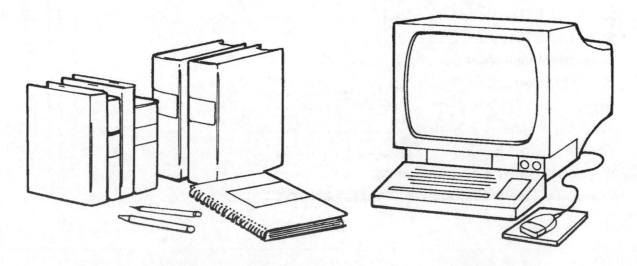

HOW TO USE THIS BOOK

The first section of *Integrating Technology into the Language Arts Curriculum* will focus on information to help you use technology as a learning tool in your classroom. This section discusses equipment, management, assessment, and suggested software.

The second section of *Integrating Technology into the Language Arts Curriculum* is devoted to lesson plans. These lesson plans focus on integrating technology into four language arts areas: Reading, Writing, Speaking, and Listening. Many of the lesson plans cover several of these areas, and could be used across the curriculum. Monthly thematic ideas are also given for slide show or hypermedia projects.

The final section of this book serves as a reference guide for future technology-assisted projects. This section names technology books and resources including a list of Web sites and URL (Uniform Resource Locator) addresses.

HARDWARE

Hardware is the term used when referring to the actual electronic machinery used for technology. When using technology in the classroom, there are many different types of hardware tools and tool combinations available to you and your students. The following list offers brief descriptions of popular hardware devices.

Computer

A computer is an electronic machine which processes data. The output is given in a way that is understandable, such as text or pictures seen on the computer monitor, or information on paper printed by the printer. A computer does basically three things: accepts data, processes data, outputs information. Virtually every computer on the market today is now a multimedia computer. A multimedia computer contains the monitor, CD-ROM drive, modem, sound card, and microphone all built into one unit. The keyboard is attached by a cord.

Monitor

Another word for the computer screen. Monitors come in several sizes including 13, 15, 17, 20, and 21 inches. Most schools use a standard 15 inch monitor with a resolution of 640 x 480 pixels.

Keyboard

A keypad with alpha, numeric, and function keys used to communicate with the computer.

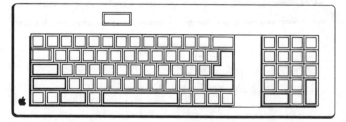

Mouse

A small hand-held device connected to the keyboard which allows you to control the position of the cursor on the screen. Move the mouse on a flat surface such as a static-free mouse pad or the top of your desk.

HARDWARE *(cont.)*

CD-ROM

CD-ROM stands for compact disk, read only memory. The CD-ROM player will read the contents of the CD-ROM and present the images onto the computer monitor.

Microphone

A device which allows you to record sounds. Microphones can be built into the computer or external devices which connect via cable.

Modem

A device which allows a computer to communicate to other computers via the telephone line. Modems are generally now built into the computer but occasionally will be external boxes. The speed of the modem is called the Baud rate. The faster the Baud rate, the faster you can access the Internet and download files.

Printer

A separate piece of hardware from the computer connected via cable. The printer takes the text, pictures, and images from the monitor and prints them onto paper. Common types of printers are laser printers, ink-jet printers, dot matrix printers, and image setters.

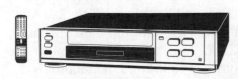

Laserdisc Player

Also known as a videodisc player, this piece of hardware is used to play laserdiscs. A laserdisc looks like a CD-ROM disc except it is larger. It is about the size of a standard long-playing phonograph record, and contains permanently stored large quantities of information in the format of text, graphics, movies, and sound. The laserdisc player is about the size of a VCR and similar in its features. You control the laserdisc either manually by choosing the appropriate buttons, or with a remote control or barcode reader.

HARDWARE *(cont.)*

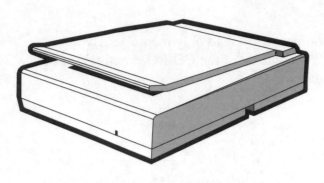

Scanner

A scanner allows you to copy an image which is outside of the computer, and then import the image back into the computer. There are two types of scanners; flatbed and handheld. A flatbed scanner works very much like a copy machine where items to be copied are placed flat onto the glass. Handheld scanners are small enough to fit into your hand and roll over the flat image while taking a "picture" of the image. Images are then saved to a floppy disk or directly onto the computer hard drive.

Digital Camera

This handy device allows you to take pictures of people, places, and events away from the computer, then later use these images for multimedia projects. A digital camera looks and operates very much like a 35 mm camera. The primary difference is the digital camera outputs images in digital form instead of photographic film. These digital images can be stored either to a floppy disk or directly on to the hard drive of the computer.

Note: *Both scanners and digital cameras are useful pieces of hardware with unique advantages. A scanner is best used when copying two-dimensional images (i.e.: student illustrations, writing samples, maps). A digital camera is best used to capture three-dimensional images (i.e.: students engaged in an activity, field trips, artwork such as sculpture, science experiments).*

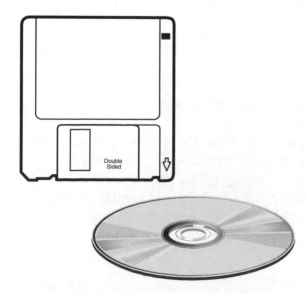

Digital Developing

Another way to capture photographs for use in student projects is through the use of digital developing. Many film developers like Kmart, and Seattle FilmWorks (A popular mail order company) will develop 35MM film on disk or photo CD-ROM. Disk developing is much less expensive than photo CD-ROM and the quality is fine for most student projects.

HARDWARE *(cont.)*

Video Camera

At one time, video cameras were quite large, heavy, and could only be held on your shoulder while recording. Now video cameras are small enough to fit into the palm of your hand. The video camera (or "camcorder," as they are often referred to) records events and activity as it occurs into a movie format and saves the images to tape. With the appropriate software and cables, you can connect the video camera to your multimedia computer, download movies, then save them as files directly onto the computer hard drive.

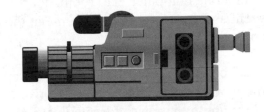

Tripod

A three-legged device which holds the video camera in place. The legs of the tripod can be adjusted to different heights. Tripods are used for long term and remote control recording.

Video Remote Control

A corded or wireless attachment that allows users to enable the camera functions without touching the camera.

TV as a Presentation Tool

Use a television as a presentation tool by connecting your computer to the TV. This is an easy and cost-effective strategy to obtain large screen projection for the classroom. There are several systems available which will allow you to connect the computer to the television. Some popular systems include: L-TV Portable and L-TV Internal Card (Focus Enhancements), TelevEyes/Plus and TelevEyes/Pro (Digital Vision), and The Presenter Mac/PC 3 (Consumer Technology). For older computer models, sometimes all that is necessary is an RF Modulator or Y-Splitter cable (both found at Radio Shack and other electronic stores).

LAB MANAGEMENT

Work on the computer lends itself well to cooperative learning. Teams of 3–5 students working at a single computer tend to produce more creative output than one single student. One idea generates another and the whole team profits. Each group should, ideally, have mixed abilities and interests. Even in a one-computer classroom, cooperative learning works. You can have groups involved in different aspects of the project, some at the computer while others are involved in essential, but non-computer modules.

An ideal computer lab configuration has learning centers. A fifteen-machine computer lab, for example, might have three groups of five computers loaded with instructional software. Five is also the usual minimum purchase for site licenses in a lab pack, so software purchases become simpler. This set up creates a lab for twenty-five students or more with only fifteen computers and as few as two printers.

An information center makes a useful addition to the lab. Place a table in front of a bulletin board. Stock the table with software manuals and post the lab schedule on the bulletin board.

Another helpful addition is the software help binder. This is where teachers can jot down information and helpful hints like:

> software glitches
>
> hardware problems
>
> ideas for using a piece of software with children
>
> student logs

One way to manage the lab is to set it up in learning centers. Teachers can then rotate their students and work with those centers that require more teacher interaction.

Independent Learning Center

One center can be set up to facilitate independent discovery learning. Games that teach language mechanics, reading, and writing skills can be installed on these computers. Be sure to pick software that matches your curriculum, is easy to use, and captures the students' interest so as to facilitate independent work.

Some suggestions include:
The Jump Start series (Knowledge Adventure)
The Blaster Series (Davidson)

Research Center

The research center can be a semi-independent area where students gather information about content that is being studied in their classroom. It is important to provide students with a structured assignment so that they can make the most out of this center.

> Software suggestions include:
> A multimedia encyclopedia like *Grolier* or *Compton's*.
> Content specific databases like *The Animals, Library of the Future, Dinosaurs* and *Internet Access*

LAB MANAGEMENT *(cont.)*

Project Center

Computers at this center should include application programs like word processors and multimedia authoring programs.

> Software suggestions include:
> *HyperStudio* (Roger Wagner Publishing)
> *Kid Pix Studio* (Broderbund)
> *The Children's Writing Center* (The Learning Company)
> *Microsoft Works* (Microsoft)
> *Claris Works* (Claris)
> Digital clip art, sounds, and video collections

Planning Center

This center includes no computers. Place a large table here with chairs and plenty of writing materials. Students can use this center to write rough drafts and plan projects.

Items to include at this center:
Pencils
Paper
Planning Sheets (see page 135)
Art supplies
Magazines
Printed copies of clip art collections

Idea Center

The idea table would have prompts for writing, inspirational material, simple science experiments, teacher and student created displays or anything that will spark ideas, curiosity, and/or interest.

LANGUAGE ARTS CLASSROOM CENTERS

Language Arts Centers in the classroom can be set up with even less equipment. Centers can work so that students rotate through four 30-minute centers. Students work in groups to do the following types of projects on a daily basis:

Literature Center:

Read literature selections, discuss literature with peers, do comprehension activities.

Publishing Center:

Write storyboards, scripts, or stories based on literature selections, write student created stories.

Props Center:

Illustrate storyboards, design animation or claymation, prepare prints to be video taped.

Multimedia Production Center:

Produce slide shows, hypermedia projects, multimedia projects, record video footage, edit recorded footage, create laserdisc presentations, research on the Internet, and prepare digital camera projects.

The Multimedia Production Center can be used throughout the school year. Students can use whatever equipment you have available in this center. This center can work with as little as one computer. Just add other technology such as video cameras, TVs with VCRs, laserdisc players, digital cameras, etc.

This type of set up works especially well with integrated units. Thematic units can be changed monthly. It works best for students to have approximately one month to complete each project.

LANGUAGE ARTS CLASSROOM CENTERS CHART

Make a classroom chart that lists the groups of students and the order of the centers in which they will rotate.

LITERATURE CENTER

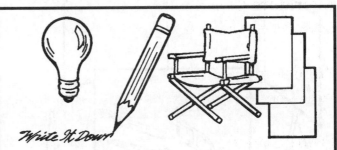

PUBLISHING CENTER

PROPS CENTER

MULTIMEDIA PRODUCTION CENTER

DIAGRAM OF LANGUAGE ARTS CENTERS SET-UP

14

PERFORMANCE-BASED

There are all types of assessment that work well with technology. You can evaluate student performance with a checklist, a rubric, or even an antecedotal record. These types of assessment not only give the student information about what he/she did on a particular project but also provide him or her with specific information about the areas that require the most improvement.

To devise an assessment of a project, it is much easier to break a project into manageable parts. These should match the educational objectives of the project.

MULTIMEDIA PRESENTATION 5-POINT RUBRIC

	5	4	3	2	1	0
Overall Presentation	The project flows well, keeps the attention of the audience, and is very interesting.	The project flows well and is interesting.	The majority of the project flows well and includes some interesting items.	The majority of the project is disjointed and the interest level is sporadic.	The project does not flow at all, is poorly presented, and has no interest whatsoever.	No response.
Text Information	The information used is accurate, well-written, and complete, with proper grammar and punctuation.	The majority of the text is accurate, uses proper grammar, and mostly flows well.	The project uses an acceptable amount of text, information is accurate, and acceptable grammar and punctuation are used.	Text information is short and inaccurate. Grammar and punctuation are mostly incorrect.	Information is missing, and grammar and punctuation are misused.	No response.
Graphics and Scanned Images	Images are used to enhance the information and support text. The placement of the images is pleasing to the eye.	Images are used to enhance the information and support text. The placement of the images is appropriate.	Images used enhance the information somewhat. The placement of the images is acceptable.	Images used have relevance to information, but not enough images are used.	No graphics or scanned images are used.	No response.

SELF-ASSESSMENT

Evaluate your performance on this project, using the following scale:

Not Yet = I did not meet the requirements.

Almost There = I was very close but fell short of meeting the requirements.

I Did It! = I met the requirements.

Above and Beyond = I went above and beyond what was required by doing something extra.

Explain why you earned that rating. Include evidence or reasons that demonstrate it.

1. I selected an appropriate topic.

   Not Yet   Almost There   I Did It!   Above and Beyond

   Why?_____

2. I did the required research or preparation.

   Not Yet   Almost There   I Did It!   Above and Beyond

   Why?_____

3. I was well prepared when it was time to work on the computer.

   Not Yet   Almost There   I Did It!   Above and Beyond

   Why?_____

4. My project has the required parts.

   Not Yet   Almost There   I Did It!   Above and Beyond

   Why?_____

5. I used creativity in my project.

   Not Yet   Almost There   I Did It!   Above and Beyond

   Why?_____

The best thing about my project is _____

I could improve my project if I _____

Things I learned doing this project were _____

I filled out this evaluation honestly.   Yes ❑   No ❑

Signature: _____   Project: _____

Date _____

SELF ASSESSMENT
JOB PERFORMANCE RECORD

Name: _____

Project: _____

Job Performance Record

Keep track of the duties you perform in your group each day you work on your project. Have the other students in your group initial each day to verify that you fulfilled your responsibilities.

Day # _____
Date: _____
Job: _____
The things I contributed to my group today were:

_____
_____

_____

Students' Initials: _____

Day # _____
Date: _____
Job: _____
The things I contributed to my group today were:

_____
_____

_____

Students' Initials: _____

Day # _____
Date: _____
Job: _____
The things I contributed to my group today were:

_____
_____

_____

Students' Initials: _____

Day # _____
Date: _____
Job: _____
The things I contributed to my group today were:

_____
_____

Students' Initials: _____

GENERAL SOFTWARE SUGGESTIONS

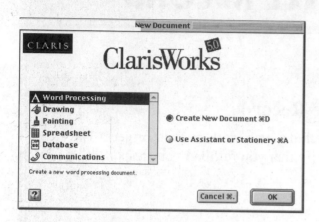

Title: *ClarisWorks*

Publisher: Claris Corporation

An integrated software package that combines word processing, painting, drawing, spreadsheet, database, and communication capabilities.

Title: *Microsoft Works*

Publisher: Microsoft Corporation

An integrated software package that combines word processing, painting, drawing, spreadsheet, database, and communication capabilities.

Title: *HyperStudio*

Publisher: Roger Wagner Publishing

Multimedia authoring software which offers the ability to bring together text, sound, graphics and video. *HyperStudio* allows for: accessing data on the Internet, creating and editing *QuickTime* movies, built-in image capture, Mac-Windows project compatibility, and a wide range of file type compatibility for graphics and sound.

Title: *Imagination Express*

Publisher: Edmark

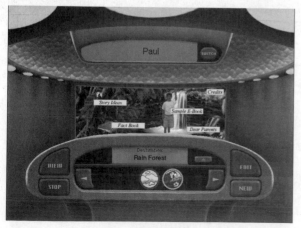

Students easily create interactive electronic books and printed stories. Each destination contains a variety of backgrounds and hundreds of stickers. The students simply drag the stickers onto the backgrounds, then add text, narration, music or sound effects. These programs also include a movie making feature which allows students to drag stamps across the screen, then replay their motion. Students can also browse through fact books which give information about each destination. Separate destinations include: Castle, Neighborhood, Rain Forest, Ocean, Pyramids, and Time Trip, U.S.A.

GENERAL SOFTWARE SUGGESTIONS *(cont.)*

Title: *Kid Pix Studio*

Publisher: Broderbund

A multimedia paint and animation program which includes six projects: Kid Pix, Moopies, SlideShow, Wacky TV, Stampimator and Digital Puppets. Students can use the SlideShow portion to create their own animated stories, photo essays, and presentations. Features include over 1300 animated and rubber stamps, 50 Wacky Brushes, and dozens of multi-color fill patterns, text tools, song clips, and sound effects.

Title: *The Print Shop*

Publisher: Broderbund

Enables users to create and print six different types of projects, including greeting cards, signs, banners, calendars, letterhead and labels. Students can choose from over 1,000 graphics to create full-page designs and layouts.

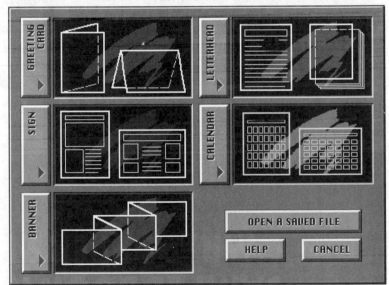

Title: *The Writing Center*

Publisher: The Learning Company

A simple word processing program that provides students with templates to create stories, newsletters, menus, letters, flyers and other text-based projects.

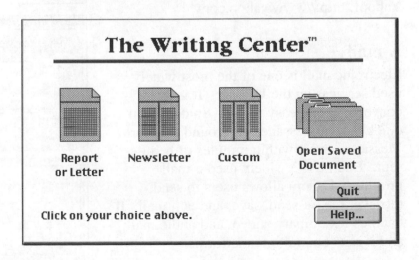

INTERNET IN THE INTERMEDIATE CLASSROOM

Internet

The Internet is the most widespread computer network. It provides many services that are useful as educational tools.

World Wide Web:

The World Wide Web (WWW) is one of the most exciting Internet services to be used for education. To access the WWW you need a WWW Browser (*Netscape, Microsoft Explorer,* etc.). These browsers interpret and display documents found on the WWW.

Links within WWW documents can take you quickly to other related documents.

Search Engines:

Search engines are helpful for researching just about any topic. The following URL addresses assist users in locating information:

Alta Vista: http://www.altavista.digital.com
Excite: http://www.excite.com
InfoSeek: http://www.Infoseek.com
Lycos: http://www.lycos.com
WebCrawler: http://webcrawler.com
Yahoo!: http://www.yahoo.com

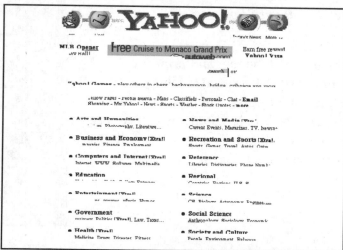

E-mail

Electronic mail is one of the most widely used services on the Internet. It is fast, convenient, and easy to use. Students can quickly send messages all around the world. Messages arrive within minutes of being sent. Eudora is a widely used e-mail program. Eudora allows users to send, retrieve, file, re-send, save, and edit mail. It handles text, binary, video, and audio mail; and it runs on multiple platforms.

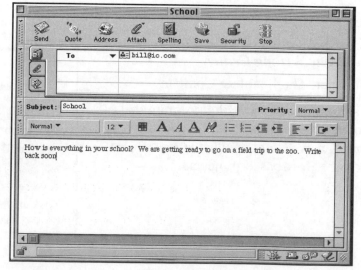

INTERNET IN THE INTERMEDIATE CLASSROOM *(cont.)*

Mailing Lists/LISTSERVS:

Mailing lists are a way for a group of people with common interests to share information. LISTSERV software has been developed to automate the administration of mailing lists. Requests for information or to subscribe (participate) or unsubscribe (drop out), are automatically handled by a central host. Teachers can subscribe to hundreds of mailing lists. One of those mailing lists is HILITES (HILITES@gsn.org). All messages sent to the HILITES list must meet a certain criteria before they are posted. This is to ensure that subscribers to HILITES mailboxes won't be flooded with inappropriate or off-subject messages. HILITES is reserved for K–12 teachers to announce learning projects which will engage students in other classes in one or more collaborative learning activities.

Collaborative Telecommunications Project Postings:

The Internet offers an effective way to teach students to both communicate and collaborate by connecting teams of students with classrooms around the world. Thousands of educational collaborative projects exists. The Global School Net (GSN) Internet Project Registry (http://www.gsh.org/gsn/proj/index.html) is designed for busy teachers searching for appropriate online projects to integrate into their classrooms. This registry is the one central place where teachers can find projects from the GSN and other organizations such as IEARN, IECC, NASA, GLOBE, Academy One, TIES, Tenet, and TERC. Projects are listed by the month in which they begin.

Newsgroups:

Newsgroups are discussion groups on all kinds of subjects. The messages are posted to the group and anyone can answer.

Internet Relay Chat (IRC):

This is an interactive communication system where users can chat with people from all over the world. Everything is typed instead of spoken. IRC is made up of topic-specific channels. When you connect to IRC, you will see a listing of the current active channels, and the topics being discussed. Teachers should use caution when letting students explore these channels.

A variety of K–12 newsgroups, and IRC projects and activities can be found at: http://www.useekufind.com/tproject.html

INTERNET LIBRARY

In this lesson, students use the Internet to find a book that they would like to read.

Grade Level: three to five

Duration: 20–30 minutes on the computer

Materials:

Internet system on a computer

URL addresses of literature sites

e-mail (for extension activities)

pencil and note paper

Procedure:

Before the Computer:

• Introduce this activity by asking the students to think about their favorite kinds of stories. Are they fantasy, biographies, science fiction, poetry, etc.? Tell them that they are going to find a good book to read using the Internet.

• Tell the students that, like their houses, every Web page on the Internet has a specific address. If the students are not familiar with how to enter the Internet address (URL) of a specific Web page, instruct students on how and where to type in a URL address in your browser. Make sure you stress the importance of typing the exact address.

On the Computer:

• Students search children's literature, using one of the following URL addresses:

Newbery Award
http://www.psi.net/chapterone/children/index.html

Children's Literature Web Guide
http://www.ucalgary.ca/~dkbrown/index.html

• Have them explore the sites and choose a list of several books that interest them.

• Students then go to the library or bookstore and find one of the books.

• Students type the appreciation of what they have read to keypal in the classroom, using e-mail or on paper. Students reply to other's appreciation.

INTERNET LIBRARY *(cont.)*

The Children's Literature Web Guide

Features

- What's New!
- **News Flash**: Newbery & Caldecott winners announced January 12, 1998 NEW
- Best Books of 1997: A Roundup of Lists from All Over NEW
- What We're Reading: Commentary on Children's Books
- Web-Traveller's Toolkit: Essential Kid Lit Websites

Discussion Boards

- Readers Helping Readers
- The Newbery/Caldecott 1998: Picks and Guesses
- Conference Bulletin Board

Quick Reference

- Children's Book Awards
- Children's Bestsellers
- The Doucette Index: Teaching Ideas for Children's Books

More Links

- Authors on the Web
- Stories on the Web
- Lots of Lists: Recommended Books
- Journals and Book Reviews
- Resources for Teachers
- Resources for Parents
- Resources for Storytellers
- Resources for Writers and Illustrators
- Digging Deeper: Research Guides and Indexes
- Internet Book Discussion Groups
- Movies and Television based on Children's Books
- Children's Literature Organizations on the Internet
- Children's Publishers and Booksellers on the Internet

About this Website

- Introduction
- Search this Site
- E-Mail the Webmaster

Internet Resources Related to Books for Children and Young Adults

Extension Activities:

- The student can present his or her appreciation of the book to the class.

- The student answers questions from his or her classmates.

- A Web page about the book can be designed by the student to share with other students who may be interested in the book.

- Students can search for keypals outside of their school with whom to communicate about their books.

Some places to look for keypals include:

http://www.keypals.com/p/keysites.html
http://impulse.hawkesbury.uws.edu.au/CPAW/

BOOK REVIEW POSTERS

In this project, students use the computer to create posters that advertise a book that they have read.

Grade Level: four to five

Duration: 20–40 minutes on the computer

Materials:
books
pencils and note paper
Book Review Organizer worksheet (page 25)
An overhead of the Sample Book Review Poster (page 26)
Word processing or desktop publishing software (see page 18)

Procedure:

Before the Computer:

- Have each student choose a book to be read and reviewed.

- Once their book has been read, each student completes the Book Review Organizer (page 25) worksheet.

- As a group, discuss the role advertising plays in the sale of a product. Have the students think of themselves as advertising agents for the books they have selected.

- The students use information from the Book Review Organizer worksheet to create a book review poster on paper.

- Show the Sample Book Review Poster (page 26) on an overhead projector or make copies for each student. Discuss whether or not they feel that it is an effective poster. Ask the students to share ideas about how the layout and content of a poster can communicate ideas.

On the Computer:

- Using word processing software or a desktop publishing program, use information from the Book Review Organizer to organize and create a book review poster. Allow students to be creative, but remind them that the purpose is to share these posters with their peers. Students must be able to give accurate information about the book.

BOOK REVIEW ORGANIZER

Title: _____

Author: _____

Genre: _____

About the Author:

_____

_____

_____

Other Books by This Author:

_____

_____

Book Summary:

_____

_____

_____

_____

Book Review:

Did you enjoy it? Was it what you expected? Would you recommend it to a friend? Why or why not?

_____

_____

_____

_____

Other Books in This Genre:

_____

_____

SAMPLE BOOK REVIEW POSTER

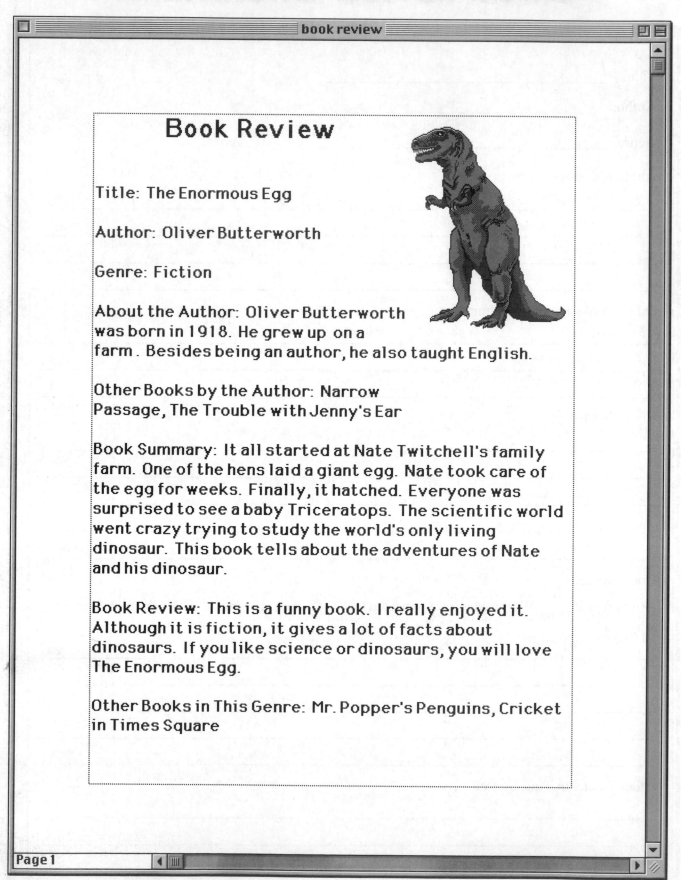

Book Review

Title: The Enormous Egg

Author: Oliver Butterworth

Genre: Fiction

About the Author: Oliver Butterworth was born in 1918. He grew up on a farm. Besides being an author, he also taught English.

Other Books by the Author: Narrow Passage, The Trouble with Jenny's Ear

Book Summary: It all started at Nate Twitchell's family farm. One of the hens laid a giant egg. Nate took care of the egg for weeks. Finally, it hatched. Everyone was surprised to see a baby Triceratops. The scientific world went crazy trying to study the world's only living dinosaur. This book tells about the adventures of Nate and his dinosaur.

Book Review: This is a funny book. I really enjoyed it. Although it is fiction, it gives a lot of facts about dinosaurs. If you like science or dinosaurs, you will love The Enormous Egg.

Other Books in This Genre: Mr. Popper's Penguins, Cricket in Times Square

BOOK REPORT SLIDE SHOWS

Almost every teacher requires some type of book report. Incorporate technology into this age old assignment to excite students by making electronic slide shows that summarize the students' books.

Grade Level: three to five

Duration: 60–120 minutes on the computer

Materials:

Books

Book Report Slide Show Organizer (Page 28, one per student)

Storyboard Organizer (Page 29, one per student)

Sample Book Report for *Mr. Popper's Penguins* (Page 30, recreated in a slide show program or copied onto a transparency for use on overhead projector)

A slide show program (See pages 18–19 for software)

Procedure:

Before the Computer:

- Individuals or groups of students read a literature selection.

- Use the Sample Book Report for *Mr. Popper's Penguins* to describe what the students should do.

- Students take notes using the Book Report Slide Show Organizer.

- Students use the Storyboard Organizer to plan four screens that include the title of the book and author, characters, setting, and summary of the book. Each screen should include a script and drawing.

On the Computer:

- Using their storyboards, students create four screens in their slide show program that include the following:

    Screen 1: Title of book and author

    Screen 2: Characters in the book with descriptions of each

    Screen 3: Setting

    Screen 4: Book Summary

- Compile the four slides into a slide show using your software and add sound and transitions as needed for effect. In order to make locating slides easier for students and teacher, each screen/slide should be saved with a different name.

- Have students preview the slide show, make changes as needed, then present it to the class.

BOOK REPORT SLIDE SHOW ORGANIZER

Directions: As you read your story, take notes in the appropriate boxes. Use this sheet to help you plan your slide show.

Title of Book	Characters
Author	

Setting	Summary

STORYBOARD ORGANIZER

Slide # _____

Words/Narration _____

_____

_____

_____

_____

Slide # _____

Words/Narration _____

_____

_____

_____

_____

Slide # _____

Words/Narration _____

_____

_____

_____

_____

Slide # _____

Words/Narration _____

_____

_____

_____

_____

SAMPLE BOOK REPORT FOR MR. POPPER'S PENGUINS

Mr. Popper's
Penguins

by

Richard & Florence Atwater

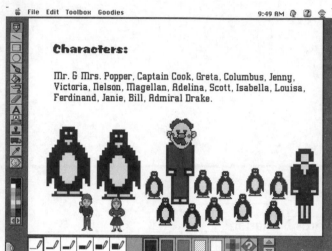

Characters:

Mr. & Mrs. Popper, Captain Cook, Greta, Columbus, Jenny, Victoria, Nelson, Magellan, Adelina, Scott, Isabella, Louisa, Ferdinand, Janie, Bill, Admiral Drake.

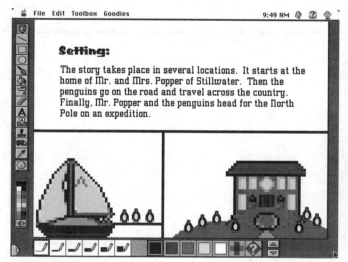

Setting:

The story takes place in several locations. It starts at the home of Mr. and Mrs. Popper of Stillwater. Then the penguins go on the road and travel across the country. Finally, Mr. Popper and the penguins head for the North Pole on an expedition.

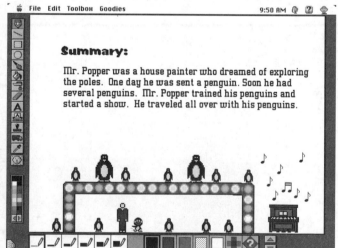

Summary:

Mr. Popper was a house painter who dreamed of exploring the poles. One day he was sent a penguin. Soon he had several penguins. Mr. Popper trained his penguins and started a show. He traveled all over with his penguins.

FACT BOOK RESEARCH

More and more students need to read, comprehend, and evaluate information. In this lesson, students use multimedia graphic clues to help them read and comprehend factual information contained on CD-ROMs.

Grade Level: three to five

Duration: 30–60 minutes on the computer

Materials:

CD-ROMs that contain content related to curriculum being studied. (Edmark's *Imagination Express* series is suggested and used for this example because of its appropriateness for the elementary grades.) Any grade-appropriate CD-ROM will work as a substitution.

Note Taking Guide (page 32) and note cards

Procedure:

Before the Computer:

- Students or teacher select a topic of interest from the *Imagination Express* series to research.

On the Computer:

- Students browse through the "Fact Book" in one of the *Imagination Express* programs. Then they click on the Main Menu of the Fact Book to see a list of chapters.

- Students can select an entry of interest from a chapter. Information can be read by the students silently or a button can be clicked to hear the page read aloud. Students then take notes on the facts to make an outline of the information..

NOTE TAKING GUIDE

Animal	Description	Habitat	Diet	Interesting Facts

STORY PYRAMID

Students will use the word processor to create a story pyramid. This strategy helps students with comprehension. It could also be used for character traits and relationships with other characters.

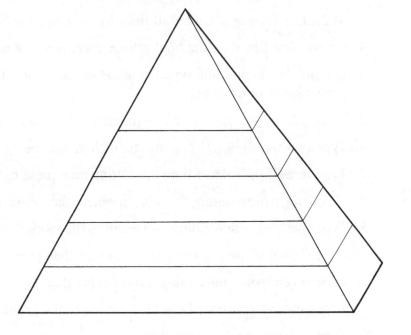

Grade Level: three to five

Duration: 20–30 minutes on the computer

Materials:

a book or story read in class

word processing software

Story Pyramid Directions (Page 34, one copy for each student or computer)

Procedure:

Before the Computer:

• Have each student read a book or story.

• Draw a story pyramid on the board for a story that all the students know. Discuss the use of descriptive words and brainstorm as a group for examples.

• Tell the students that they will be using the computer to create a story pyramid. Pass out and review the Story Pyramid Directions (Page 34). Have the students fill in the directions that are missing specific to the software that they will be using.

On the Computer:

• Have the students create a story pyramid using the Story Pyramid Directions page. The pyramid includes eight lines. The first line consists of one word, the second line has two words, the third line has three words, and so on. Students type each line and press return. If the centering alignment tool is being used, the writing will be in the shape of a pyramid when completed.

Extension activities:

• Use the file that each student created as a word bank for writing a summary of the story. Have the students copy and paste the words in the pyramid into their summary of the story.

STORY PYRAMID DIRECTIONS

1. Start your word processing software and make a new document by choosing new document.
2. Make the document center all lines by choosing the center options.
3. On the first line type the book title and press return or enter.
4. On line the second line type the name of the author then insert three to four blank lines by pressing return or enter.
5. Next type in the name of the main character then press return or enter.
6. Type two words describing the main character then press return or enter.
7. Type three words describing the setting then press return or enter.
8. Type four words stating the story problem then press return or enter.
5. Type five words describing one event in the story then press return or enter.
6. Type six words describing a second event then press return or enter.
7. Type seven words describing a third event then press return or enter.
8. Type eight words describing the solution to the problem then press return or enter twice.
9. Type in your name and the date.
10. Print your story pyramid.

_____

Book Title

_____

Author

_____,

_____, _____,

_____, _____, _____,

_____, _____, _____, _____,

_____, _____, _____, _____, _____,

_____, _____, _____, _____, _____, _____,

_____, _____, _____, _____, _____, _____, _____,

_____, _____, _____, _____, _____, _____, _____, _____,

TELECOMMUNICATIONS WRITING EXCHANGE

In this lesson, the teacher takes a writing lesson that has been successful for her or him in the past and uses it as a basis for a collaborative telecommunications project which involves the exchange of students' written information. This is a great way to motivate students to read and write.

Grade Level: three to five

Duration: Depends on project developed

Materials:

Depends on project developed

Procedure:

Before the Computer:

• Assign a story, essay, report or other writing project to your students. It is best to use a project or lesson that has been successful in the past. Tell the students that they will be exchanging their writing with other classes from different parts of the country/world so they will need to be extra careful and clear when writing. Some ideas might include:

> Observations of a piece of art
>
> Autobiographies
>
> Science experiment reports
>
> Step-by-step directions
>
> Interviews
>
> Historical newspapers
>
> Math word problems
>
> Literature character traits
>
> Collaborate on songs

• Post the project on a Web Page such as Global SchoolHouse (http://www.gsh.org/gsn/) or contact HILITES (HILITES@gsn.org), the oldest listserv on the Internet devoted exclusively to project-based classroom learning projects. Ask for other classes to take part in the writing exchange. You will need the following information.

Project:

Name of your project

Date:

Give the starting and ending dates of the complete project. Leave at least four weeks before the start of the project to permit enough people to respond to your call for collaboration.

TELECOMMUNICATIONS WRITING EXCHANGE *(cont.)*

Purpose:

In 2–3 sentences give a brief summary of the purpose of the project. What will students who participate in this project learn?

Subjects:

State the curriculum areas which will be addressed by this project. Most projects are multidisciplinary. List as many as apply.

Grade level:

Indicate the appropriate grade levels for the project.

Summary:

Briefly describe the project. This paragraph should catch the interest of your readers. Indicate the number of classrooms or participants that you wish to work with.

Project Coordinator:

Give your name and e-mail address. You may wish to include your school mailing address and phone number.

How to register:

Provide complete instructions for registering with you to complete this project. Don't forget to include your e-mail address. You may want to request all or some of the following information:

> Your full name:
>
> Your e-mail address:
>
> Your school:
>
> District:
>
> School address:
>
> School voice phone:
>
> Home voice phone:
>
> Grade(s) taught:
>
> Subject(s):

Time line:

Break down the project into very specific steps with dates, including starting and ending dates where relevant. This should in effect summarize all of the important steps of the project described below.

Complete project outline and procedures:

Describe the project in greater detail. Make an effort to be specific regarding who does what: what the other teachers and students do; what you do. This description should give participants a clear idea of what you will expect of them, and they of you.

AUTHOR RESEARCH

Students love to find out about the authors of their favorite books. The Internet now allows them to read about those authors and sometimes even correspond with them.

Grade Level: three to five

Duration: 20–30 minutes

Materials:
Internet access,
note taking materials

Procedure:

Before the Computer:

- Each student should select an author to learn about.

- Discuss the use of Search Engines. Show students how to do a keyword search by typing in a keyword in the appropriate box, then clicking on search.

On the Computer:

- Students experiment with using search engines to find their favorite authors. Some students may have better luck using the following addresses:

Yahoo's Children's Literature Area

http://www.yahoo.com/Arts/Humanities/Literature/Genres/Children_s/Authors/

Children's Literature Web Guide

http://www.ucalgary.ca/~dkbrown/index.html

- Students can take notes on interesting facts about the selected author.

Many authors have their publishers' addresses on the Internet, and some have their own Web pages and e-mail addresses. Students can try to find an address to write or e-mail their favorite authors. A good place to get started is Judy Blume's Home Base. This Web page gives students all kinds of information about her famous books like Superfudge. *She also gives students writing tips for their own stories. The page is located at: http://www.judyblume.com/home.html*

CANDY PRODUCTION FLOW CHART

The students will be able to formulate a flow chart showing the process involved in making candy coated chocolate.

Grade Level: three to five

Duration: 60 minutes

Materials:

Internet access, pencils, note taking materials, drawing paper, a paint program

Procedure:

Before the Computer:

- On the chalkboard, illustrate a flow chart showing how a peanut butter and jelly sandwich would be made.

- Discuss the importance of not leaving out details. For example, talk about what the sandwich might be like if no directions were given on how to spread the peanut butter.

- As a group, have students make a flow chart. How to brush teeth is a good example.

On the Computer:

Direct students to the M & Ms Web Site:

> URL: http://www.m-ms.com/factory/fact2.html

- Students go through the tour of the M & Ms factory. Tell students to take notes. Have them look for all of the steps involved in making the famous candy.

After the Computer:

- On drawing paper, students create a flow chart showing the process involved in making M & Ms.

- Students may want to recreate the flow chart using a paint program.

- Have students go back to the Web Site when they finish to see whether they left out any important details in the process.

- Discuss how M & Ms might taste if an important direction were left out.

STOP ACTION STORY ANIMATION

Video cameras are many times an easily accessible yet under used tool in the classroom. In this project, students use stop-motion photography to portray a short story or poem.

Grade Level: four to five

Duration: 60–120 minutes preparation time, 60-120 minutes recording and editing

Materials:

video camera with a tripod, storyboard (one per team, see page 78), construction paper, and art supplies

Before the Video Process:

- Team students in groups of 2–3 and read a short story or poem independently or in class.

- Have groups work together to do storyboard depicting the major scene that they will put in their video.

- The students should then divide up the job of creating each illustration in the storyboard. Be sure the illustrations are drawn dark as video taping tends to wash out the drawings. Cut out characters that will be animated. Be sure to make a title page.

During the Video Process:

- Tape the illustrations to a wall.

- Set up the video camera on the tripod. Angle the lens to view the object to be animated.

- Use a remote control to record for 2–3 seconds and pause.

- Move the object a small amount, being careful to move only the part you wish to animate.

- Record for 2–3 seconds and pause.

- Move the object a small amount again.

- Record and repeat procedure until you have reached the desired effect.

- Audio dub sound or music over the video tape.

GROUP CLAYMATION AND ANIMATION COMPREHENSION CHECK

Tips:

- Experiment with your camera, but try filming each frame for two seconds–stop–move object slightly and repeat over and over.

- Always use a tripod.

- Always check the camera view finder before pressing record. Make sure all hands are out of the way.

- Use video camera remote control to help eliminate unwanted camera movement.

- Tape down your background drawings so they cannot be moved. Drafting tape will allow you to remove the tape later without ruining the picture.

- Assign jobs so everyone knows what role to play.

- Don't stop recording too soon; it takes a lot of recording to make even a short video.

Simple Stop Motion Projects to Get Started On:

- seeds sprouting/plants growing

- explorer ships sailing

- food chain/smallest fish to largest fish

- jumping jack characters

Some Fun Claymation Ideas:

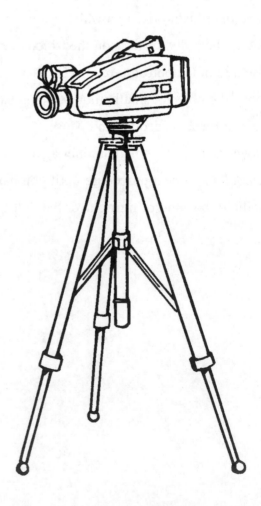

- snakes crawling

- dancing dinosaurs

- whale tales

- funny faces

- rocking chair

- egg cracking open

- dancing gold miner

- insect metamorphosis

- cars racing

- swimming octopus or jellyfish

- characters jumping rope

- moving skeletons

- ducks in a pond

- moving action figures

40

STORY MENUS

Order up! In this project students create menus that reflect details gained from reading stories and books.

Grade Level: three to five

Duration: 60 minutes on the computer

Materials:

stories or books, sample menus, pencils, Menu Organizer (Page 42), word processing software (See page 18), Sample Menu for *James and the Giant Peach* (See page 43)

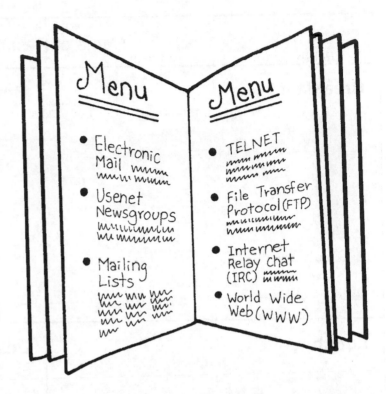

Procedure:

Before the Computer:

- Have individuals or groups of students read a story or book.

- As a group, examine a variety of menus from local restaurants. Look for things that they have in common. Also look for details that make the menus stand apart from one another.

- Brainstorm four ways to incorporate character names, story settings, and plot into the names of food items. Use the Sample Menu for *James and the Giant Peach* (page 43) as a menu example.

- Students use the Menu Organizer to plan a menu based on details from the story or book that was read.

- It is a good idea to make a template for the project ahead of time. Do this by creating a word processing document with columns and margins set up for the students. Save this file with a unique name and make sure that the students do not save over the original template. Many programs allow you to save the document as a template or lock it so as not to allow saving over it.

On the Computer:

- Using their Menu Organizer as a rough guide, have the students create their menu in the word processing software.

- Have them experiment with different font styles and sizes for emphasis, and to enhance the visual effects of the menu.

- Encourage the addition of graphics, if appropriate.

MENU ORGANIZER

Name of Restaurant

Breakfast	Beverages
Lunch	**Desserts**
Dinner	**Specials**

SAMPLE MENU FOR JAMES AND THE GIANT PEACH

James' Peach Palace
Based on the Book James & the Giant Peach

BREAKFAST
Scrambled Peaches (Fresh peaches lightly tossed) $2.50
Toasted Peaches (2 peach halves served on English muffins $1.50
Glow Worm's Peach Pancakes(2 pancakes topped with a green gummy worms)...$2.50

LUNCH
Centipede's Submarine Sandwich (Cut into 42 sections)................$3.00
Shark Stew..$3.50

DINNER
Sea Gull's Surprise (Fresh seafood catch of the day)....................$3.50
Hot Noodles Made with Poodles (The Centipede's favorite!)............$4.00
Earthworm's Spaghetti (Thick, pink & juicy with no bones)............$5.50

DRINKS..All drinks **$1.00** each.
Peach Juice
Aunt Spiker's Lemonade
Miss Spider's Cider
Cloud Men Coffee (Fresh coffee topped with a fluffy cloud of cream)

DESSERT
Aunt Sponge Cake...$2.00
James' New York Cheese Cake..$1.50
Old Green Grasshopper Pie..$2.50

ENDANGERED ANIMAL RESEARCH

The Internet provides a wealth of knowledge about endangered animals. In this project, students use the Internet to research endangered animals. In the next lesson (Page 46), students use their research to create a multimedia report.

Grade Level: three to five

Duration: 60–120 minutes on the computer.

Materials:

Internet connection, Endangered Animal Report Note Cards Sheet, *HyperStudio* Planning Sheet, *HyperStudio*

Procedure:

Before the Computer:

- Students select an audience and a topic.

On the Internet:

- Students search for information on the Internet about their selected animal. The sites listed below may be a good place to start.

  The World Conservation Union's List Site: http://www.wcmc.org.uk/data/database.rl_anml_combo.html

  Endangered Species Act Home Page: http://kingfish.ssp.nmfs.gov/tmcintyr/esahome.html

  Sea World's Animal Information Database: http://www.bev.net/education/SeaWorld

  Monterey Bay Aquarium: http://www.mbayaq.org/

- Using information found on the Internet, students fill out the Endangered Animal Report Note Cards Sheet.

ENDANGERED ANIMAL REPORT NOTE CARDS

Directions: As you research, take notes on the topics below.

Name of Animal _____

Name and Description:

Why It Is Endangered:

Where It Lives (Habitat)

What It Eats (Diet)

Enemies

Interesting Facts

ENDANGERED ANIMAL RESEARCH MULTIMEDIA REPORT

Grade Level: three to five

Duration: 120–240 minutes on the computer.

Materials:

Internet connection, Endangered Animal Report Note Cards Sheet, *HyperStudio* or similar program (see page 19), Planning Sheet

Procedure:

Before the Computer:

The students should:

- Research the information needed for their presentation. (See Endangered Animal Research, page 44)

- Gather resources such as clip art, photos, quotes, Web links, etc.

- Select information from the Endangered Animal Report Note Cards to plan a four to six card stack on the animal.

- Design a stack using the Endangered Animal Planning Sheet.

On the Computer:

- Help the students budget their time on the computer by pre-planning all the cards in their stack. It is best to require that they complete a set number of cards or slides per time on the computer. Students who have pre-planned should be able to complete a card in about 20–30 minutes.

- Have the students start by creating a background for their cards. Have them use the same background for all the cards in the stack. This will save time. This can be done by the teacher ahead of time to save the students time on the computer.

After the Computer:

- Present the stack to the class or record the stack onto video tape for others to view.

ENDANGERED ANIMAL PLANNING SHEET

Title Card

Buttons/Links: _____

Notes (Text/Sounds/Animations): _____

Card 1

Buttons/Links: _____

Notes (Text/Sounds/Animations): _____

Card 2

Buttons/Links: _____

Notes (Text/Sounds/Animations): _____

Card 3

Buttons/Links: _____

Notes (Text/Sounds/Animations): _____

Card 4

Buttons/Links: _____

Notes (Text/Sounds/Animations): _____

Card 5

Buttons/Links: _____

Notes (Text/Sounds/Animations): _____

SAMPLE ENDANGERED ANIMAL MULTIMEDIA RESEARCH REPORT

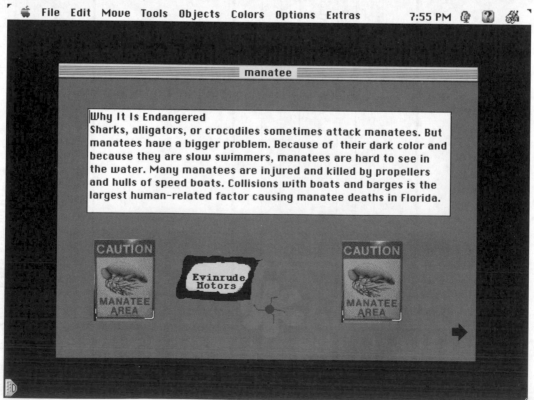

KEYPALS

Use the Internet to locate a writing buddy from across the country or around the world. Although this is the most basic type of online correspondence, it gives students the opportunity to share personal experiences with their peers. Students must concentrate on communicating an idea clearly in written form.

Grade Level: four to five

Duration: Varies

Materials:

Internet and e-mail access

Procedure:

Before the Computer:

- Find a class or individuals who would like to communicate regularly. If you are studying another culture, you might want to put in a request with Intercultural E-Mail Classroom Connection. To find keypals, log on to a keypal contacts page such as :

    http://www.ozemail.com.au/~reed/global/keypal.html

    or

    Intercultural E-Mail Classroom Connection:
    http://www.stolaf.edu/network/iecc

- Brainstorm as a group to think of questions to ask keypals. Encourage students to think of information about themselves or their community to tell their keypals.

- Have the students write the letters in class and peer edit them for content and mechanics.

On the Computer:

- The students then type the letters into an e-mail message and send them to the keypals. If students do not have e-mail accounts, they can send the letters with the teacher's e-mail account and have the student put his or her name in the subject line.

Teacher Note: Many teachers like to get involved in Learning Circles where two or more classrooms e-mail each other concerning a common theme which is being taught simultaneously. This can involve everything from sharing research to insights. AT&T has created a Learning Circle Teacher's Guide which can be found at:

                        http://www.att.com/education/lcguide/

Electronic Mentors are another way to get students involved with using e-mail. Students can contact subject matter experts with their questions. A good source for this is:

                    http://www.askanexpert.com/askanexpert/ask.html

COLLABORATIVE STORIES

Keypals can be utilized for many different activities. This activity allows students from different parts of the world to collaborate on the writing of a story. Students begin a story and send it to a keypal. The keypal adds to it and returns it for future writing.

Grade Level: four to five

Duration: Varies depending on length of story

Materials:

E-mail access, keypals

Procedure:

Before the Computer:

- Brainstorm for details to make the beginning of an exciting story.

- Students write a rough draft of a story starter on paper.

- Locate keypals with which students can communicate.
  Sites to find keypals include:

  http://www.keypals.com/p/keysites.html
  and
  http://impulse.hawkesburry.uws.edu.au/CPAW/

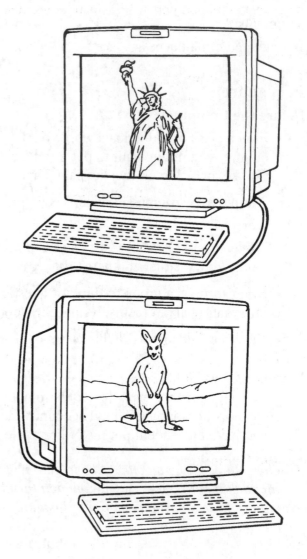

On the Computer:

- Have students type story starters into an e-mail program and send it to their keypals.

- The students ask their keypals to complete the story and send it back via e-mail for reading.

- This can be continued until the students complete the story.

Teacher Note: *Another twist to this lesson is to have keypals impersonate famous or historical individuals. One keypal thinks of questions to ask the famous person, while the other keypal takes on the role of that person. This is a good way to get students involved in the writing of historical fiction.*

PERSONAL NEWSPAPER

Students love to see their names in newspapers. Help them make the headlines by creating a newspaper about themselves.

Grade Level: three to five

Duration: 60 minutes on the computer

Materials:

newspapers, paper, pencil, Personal Newspaper Planning Sheet (Page 52), word processing software

Procedure:

Before the Computer:

- Have the students bring in sample newspapers and newsletters.

- Discuss the different types of articles in a newspaper such as local, state, national, international, humorous, sports, weather, features, etc. Also discuss other sections of a newspaper such as comics, classifieds, advertisements, etc.

- Go over the parts of a good news story. Make sure to cover the following essential items:

    A news story contains facts.

    News articles almost always include the 5 w's (Answering the questions—who, what, where, when, and why).

- Practice writing news stories as a class and individually.

- Discuss autobiographical writing. Instruct students that they are going to create an autobiographical newspaper.

- Brainstorm for types of articles that students can write about themselves. Ideas might include articles about their family, sports teams that they play on, pets, hobbies, etc.

- Have students complete the Personal Newspaper Planning Sheet and plan the layout of the newspaper.

On the Computer:

- Students type several articles about different aspects of their lives.

- Columns and graphics should be added as desired.

Teacher Note: *You may want to have students see the Newsday Project in which students produce newspapers online. The project is located at: http://www.gsn.org*

PERSONAL NEWSPAPER
PLANNING SHEET

Directions: Fill in the boxes below to help you create a newspaper all about YOU!

Sports or Activities

Who: _____

_____

What: _____

_____

Where: _____

_____

When: _____

_____

Why: _____

_____

Hobbies or Interests

Who: _____

_____

What: _____

_____

Where: _____

_____

When: _____

_____

Why: _____

_____

Sports or Activities

Who: _____

_____

What: _____

_____

Where: _____

_____

When: _____

_____

Why: _____

_____

Family and Pet Information

Who: _____

_____

What: _____

_____

Where: _____

_____

When: _____

_____

Why: _____

_____

SAMPLE PERSONAL NEWSPAPER

Haley's Herald

All About Me

My name is Haley. I am ten years old and I am in fourth grade. I have brown hair and blue eyes. I live with my mom, dad, and brother.

Favorite Sport

My favorite sport is swimming. I like to try different dives. I also like to race across the pool. One day, I would like to be in the Olympics.

Pets

I love animals! I have several pets. I have a cat named Storm, a dog named Chemo, a tortoise named Shelby, and a whole bunch of fish. I would like to be a veterinarian when I grow up.

Hobbies

I like to work on the computer for fun. I play games, write stories, and look for stuff on the Internet!

FAIRY TALE SLIDE SHOWS

Students create colorful fairy tale slide shows using *Kid Pix Studio* or another slide show program.

Grade Level: three to five

Duration: 60–120 minutes on the computer

Materials:

Fairy Tale Planning Sheet, pencil, crayons, paper, Storyboard Planning Sheet, *Kid Pix Studio* or comparable program (See page 19)

Procedure:

Before the Computer:

- Read several fairy tales aloud to the class. Discuss important elements of the stories.

- Give students the Fairy Tale Planning Sheet to develop characters, a setting, a problem and a solution for their own fairy tale.

- Have students write a fairy tale on paper.

- Students use the Storyboard Planner to turn the fairy tale into a slide show. Tell students that each slide should include graphics and text or narration. For each slide idea the students should pre-plan on paper:

  a picture to represent each slide.

  a script for each slide.

On the Computer:

- Have students create the desired number of slides in *Kid Pix* or other appropriate software.

- Each slide should be saved with a different name such as Tale1, Tale 2, etc.

- Use the slide show feature to place the creations in the appropriate order.

- Add narration or appropriate sound effects to each slide.

- Select an appropriate transition for each slide.

- Save and play the completed slide show. Record the slide show onto video tape or print out on paper if desired.

SAMPLE FAIRY TALE SLIDE SHOW

SAMPLE FAIRY TALE PAGES

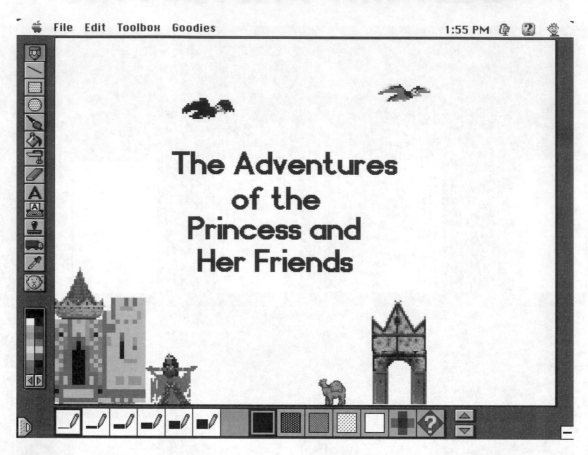

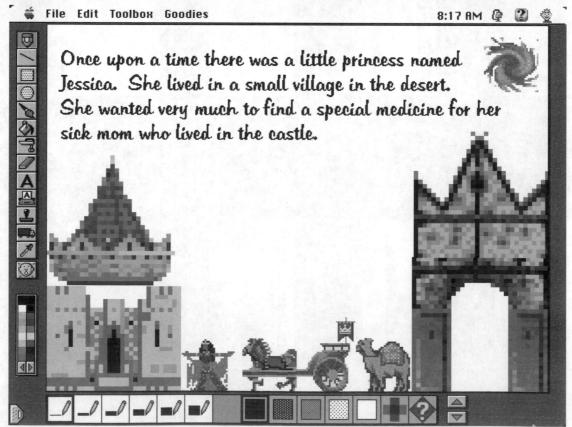

SAMPLE FAIRY TALE PAGES *(cont.)*

One day she left her castle to look for the medicine. Soon she met a camel named Mel. He told her how to get through the dangerous desert. Together they traveled for days.

Finally, they reached the enchanted forest. They came upon a deer named Dee Dee. She showed them how to get out of the forest safely.

SAMPLE FAIRY TALE PAGES *(cont.)*

The group came to a terrible sea. They had no way to get across. A beautiful mermaid offered to guide them safely across to the island that had the special medicine.

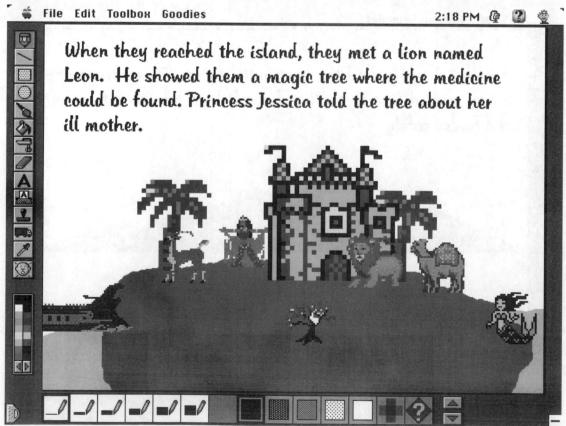

When they reached the island, they met a lion named Leon. He showed them a magic tree where the medicine could be found. Princess Jessica told the tree about her ill mother.

FAIRY TALE PLANNING SHEET

Name: _____

Date: _____

Directions: Draw slides for your fairy tale.

Characters	**Setting**
Problem	**Solution**

LASERDISC DESCRIPTIVE WRITING

Pictures can spur students' creative sides and help develop vocabulary and descriptive writing skills. If your school has a laserdisc player and appropriate laserdiscs, use the pictures as writing prompts. Just about any laserdisc can be used for this assignment, so look for frames that will enhance the curriculum.

Grade Level: three to five

Duration: 30 minutes

Materials:

laserdisc player, laserdiscs, paper, pencil, Five Senses Brainstorming Sheet (Page 61)

Procedure:

- Before class, search through laser disc footage and select a frame that fits into your curriculum.

- Discuss adjectives as a whole group. Make a list of descriptive words from the discussion.

- Put in the laserdisc and locate the appropriate frame.

- Have students examine the laserdisc frame shown on the TV carefully.

- Pass out the Five Senses Brainstorming Sheet.

- Students should use their observation skills and the Five Senses Brainstorming Sheet to think of words to describe the laserdisc frame.

- Each student should then write a descriptive paragraph about the frame.

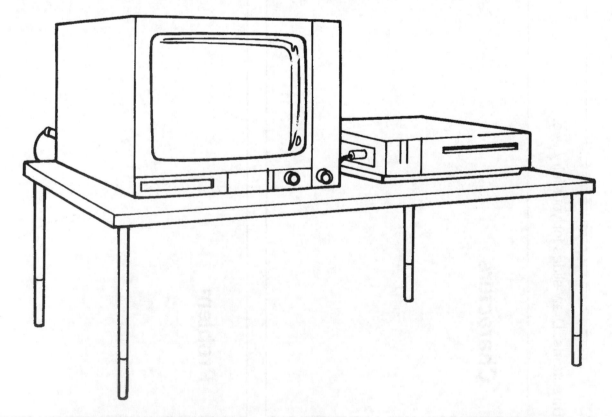

THE FIVE SENSES BRAINSTORMING SHEET

Directions: Use your five senses to list adjectives that tell about the scene. Be as descriptive as possible.

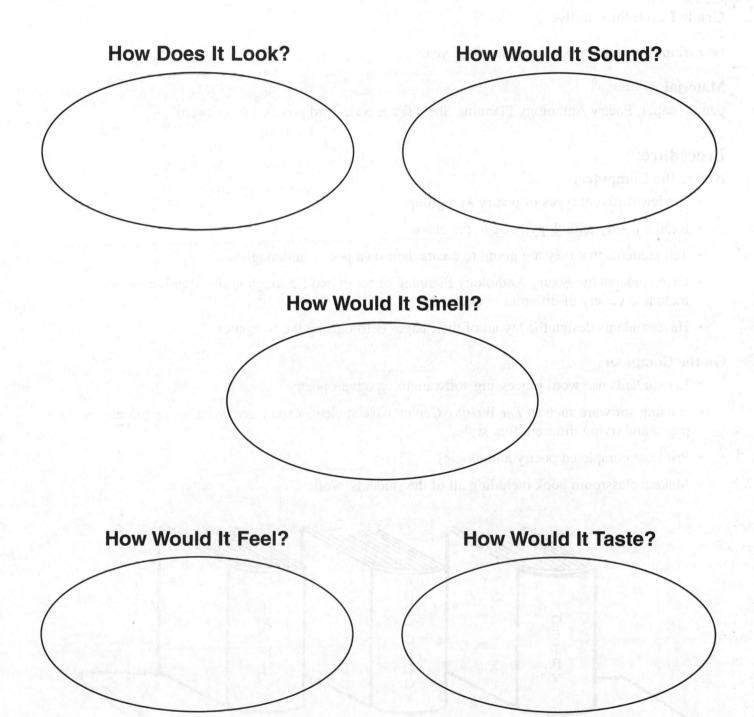

How Does It Look?

How Would It Sound?

How Would It Smell?

How Would It Feel?

How Would It Taste?

POETRY ANTHOLOGIES

Compile poems written in class into a poetry anthology page or book. You may want to have students visit some poetry Web sites before starting this project. A good page to start with is:

Positively Poetry

http://iquest.com/~e-media/kv/poetry.html

Grade Level: three to five

Duration: Several periods throughout the year

Materials:

pencil, paper, Poetry Anthology Planning Sheet (Page 63), word processing software

Procedure:

Before the Computer:

- Review different types of poetry as a group.

- Read a poetry anthology book to the class.

- Tell students that they are going to create their own poetry anthologies.

- Give students the Poetry Anthology Planning Sheet to make a rough draft. Remind them to include a variety of different poem types.

- Have students design the layout of their pages before using the computer.

On the Computer:

- Let students use word processing software to type their poetry.

- If using software such as *The Writing Center,* have students experiment with using columns on the pages and trying different font styles.

- Print out completed poetry anthologies.

- Make a classroom book including all of the students' work.

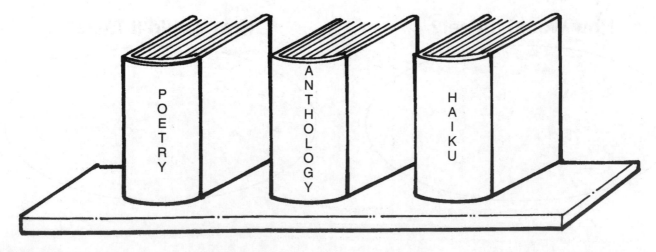

POETRY ANTHOLOGY PLANNING SHEET

Name Poem

A name poem describes a person. The first letter in each line spells out the name of the person about whom the poem is written.

Diamonte

Diamonte poems create the shape of a diamond and follow these rules:

Line 1: A noun

Line 2: 2 adjectives that describe the noun

Line 3: 3 verbs ending in -ing that tell what the noun does

Line 4: 2 more adjectives that describe the noun

Line 5: A synonym for line 1

Cinquain

A cinquain is a five line verse that follows this form:

Line 1: 1 noun of 2 syllables

Line 2: 4 syllables (describing line 1)

Line 3: 6 syllables (telling action for line 1)

Line 4: 8 syllables (expressing feeling or giving information about line 1)

Line 5: Another 2 syllable noun

Limericks

A limerick is a short, silly poem that is usually five lines long. Limericks follow these rules:

Lines 1,2, and 5 rhyme

Lines 1,2, and 5 have 8,9, or 10 beats.

Lines 3 and 4 rhyme

Lines 3 and 4 have 5, 6, or 7 beats

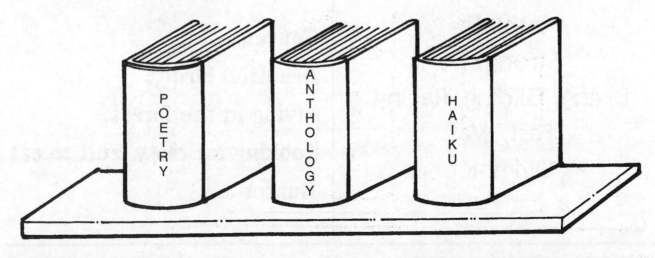

SAMPLE POETRY ANTHOLOGY

Poetry by Ashley

MY NAME POEM

A - ATHLETIC
S - SMART
H - HAPPY
L - LOVABLE
E - ENERGETIC
Y - YOUNG

Space Dog Limerick

There once was a dog from outer space

Who had a very ugly face.

He had very fast speed

and was always in the lead

So he entered the very ugly dog race.

Diamonte Poem

Athlete
Strong, Fit
Diving, Gliding, Racing
Fast, Wet
Swimmer

Toucan Cinquain

Toucan
Beautiful bird
Flying in the forest
Looking for tasty fruit to eat
Hunter

"CHOOSE YOUR OWN ENDING" ADVENTURE STORY

Students will write their own mystery or adventure story with different endings and create that story in *Hyperstudio*.

Grade Level: four to five

Duration: 60–180 minutes on the computer

Materials:

"Choose Your Own Ending" Planning Sheet (Page 70), "Choose Your Own Ending" Branching Guide (Page 71)

Procedure:

Before the Computer:

- Read a mystery story and discuss its elements. Tell students that surprise is the most important element.

- Tell students that they are going to write their own mystery or adventure stories.

- Give students the "Choose Your Own Ending" Planning Sheet to assist them with a problem and several possible solutions for their stories.

- Encourage students to think of a setting that has unusual details and adds a hint of suspense.

- Students then use the "Choose Your Own Ending" Branching Guide to plan out a *HyperStudio* stack that tells the story.

- Discuss basic design features for *HyperStudio* cards. Encourage the creative use of background colors, clip art, and graphics.

- If needed, show students how to add buttons. Have them follow the steps in the program to get the buttons to link to the appropriate cards.

On the Computer:

- Students begin by creating a title card that establishes the plot of the story. They should include at least two buttons that lead the story in two directions.

- Students continue adding cards that give different twists to the story. Each card should always include at least two buttons with different consequences.

- Make sure students include other buttons that link back to previous cards so the reader can try all of the options.

- Share the stories with the class.

"CHOOSE YOUR OWN ENDING" ADVENTURE STORY SAMPLE

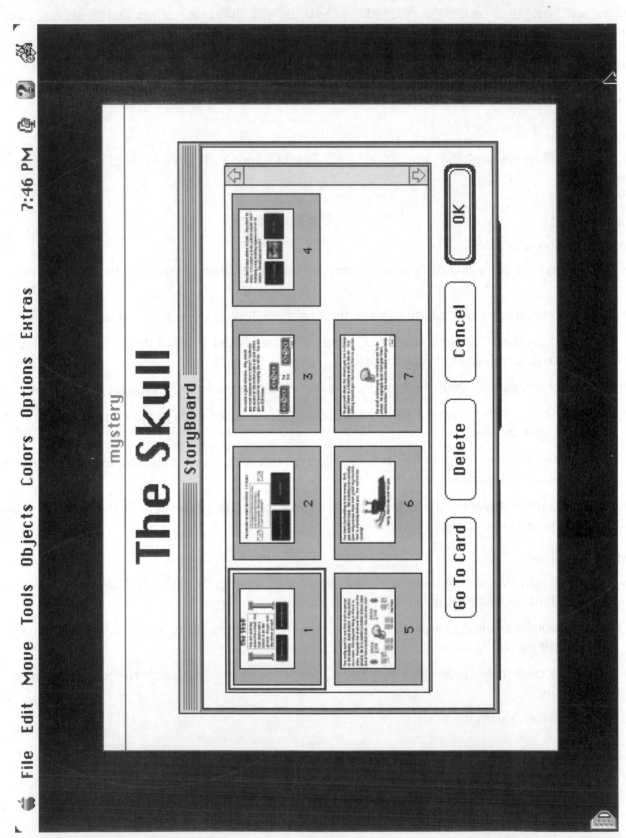

"CHOOSE YOUR OWN ENDING" ADVENTURE STORY SAMPLE *(cont.)*

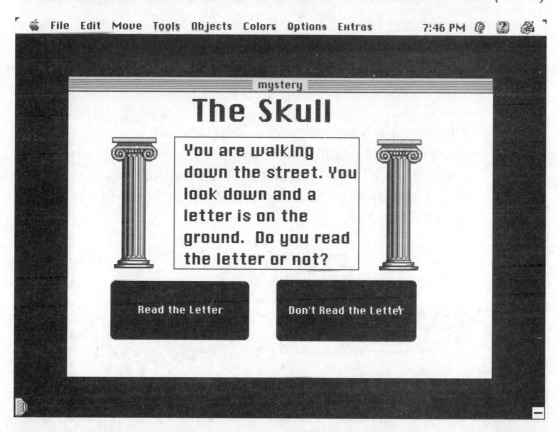

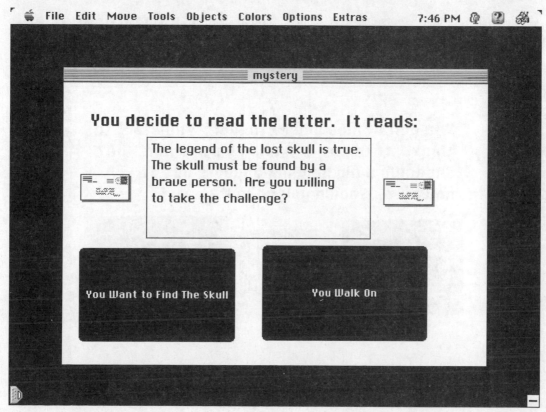

"CHOOSE YOUR OWN ENDING" ADVENTURE STORY SAMPLE *(cont.)*

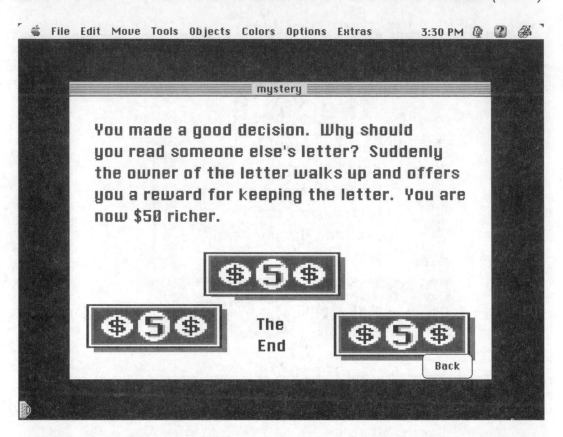

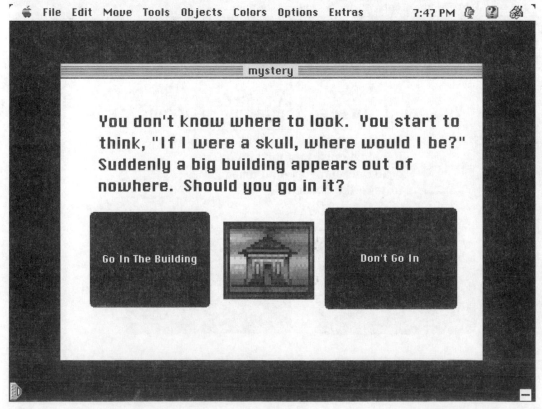

"CHOOSE YOUR OWN ENDING" ADVENTURE STORY SAMPLE *(cont.)*

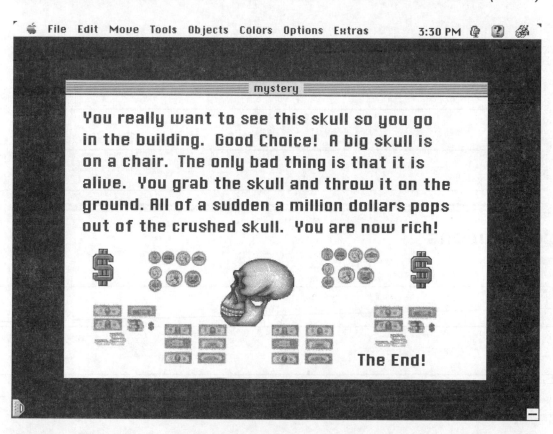

File Edit Move Tools Objects Colors Options Extras   3:30 PM

mystery

You really want to see this skull so you go in the building. Good Choice! A big skull is on a chair. The only bad thing is that it is alive. You grab the skull and throw it on the ground. All of a sudden a million dollars pops out of the crushed skull. You are now rich!

The End!

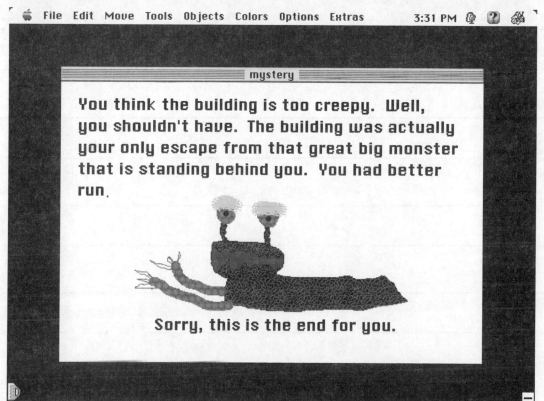

File Edit Move Tools Objects Colors Options Extras   3:31 PM

mystery

You think the building is too creepy. Well, you shouldn't have. The building was actually your only escape from that great big monster that is standing behind you. You had better run.

Sorry, this is the end for you.

"CHOOSE YOUR OWN ENDING" PLANNING SHEET

Problem

_____

_____

_____

Possible Solutions

1. _____

_____

2. _____

_____

3. _____

_____

4. _____

_____

5. _____

_____

6. _____

_____

"CHOOSE YOUR OWN ENDING" BRANCHING GUIDE

Name: _____

Date: _____

IMAGINATION EXPRESS STORIES

Edmark's *Imagination Express* is a series of software that allows students to learn specific content, then write professional looking books and multimedia reports about the information that they have learned. Students can use it to write everything from simple stories to elaborate books.

Grade Level: three to five

Duration: Varies depending on length of story

Materials:

paper, pencil, *Imagination Express,* paper to print or video tape to record

Procedure:

Before the Computer:

- As a whole group, review basic story elements. Remind students that a good story should have a beginning, a middle, and an end.

- Also as a whole group, go through samples of stickers and backgrounds in the program before beginning to write. Let students see the options that are available in the *Imagination Express* program that is chosen for the project.

- Once students are familiar with the program, they should select a topic about which to write.

- A rough draft for the story should be written on paper before using the computer.

On the Computer:

Students should:

- Browse through the backgrounds, stickers, and fonts, then select an appropriate background for the first scene.

- Select a decorative text border or choose the option that allows you to type the story directly over the background.

- Type the text for the first scene of the story and drag appropriate stickers onto the background. Use the movie making feature to animate the stickers if desired.

- Add sound, narration, or music. Repeat with additional scenes until story is complete.

- Print out story pages to make a book or record the scenes onto videotape for TV viewing.

SAMPLE IMAGINATION EXPRESS PAGES

The Secret of the Sphinx

SAMPLE IMAGINATION EXPRESS PAGES *(cont.)*

One day in the Egyptian desert, a boy named Sico saw a beautiful sphinx. The beautiful thing about it was that the eyes were giant rubies.

"I AM" VIDEO POETRY

This simple poem is a great way to incorporate video into writing. It is an excellent tool for autobiographical writing and works equally as well to highlight characters from a story.

Grade Level: three to five

Duration: 60 minutes recording time

Materials:

school photographs or drawings of students, magazine pictures, video camera, tripod, video remote control, videotape, video transfer box or vertical surface and tape

Procedure:

Before the Video Process:

- Students complete the "I Am" poem in writing.

- Have students search for personal photographs, magazine pictures, or create drawings to illustrate each line of the poem.

- Organize the photographs or pictures so they are in the correct order for the poem.

- Have students practice reading the poem orally so that it is familiar to them.

During the Video Process:

- Use a video transfer box or tape the first picture to a vertical surface.

- Using a video camera with a tripod, zoom the lens to frame the picture.

- Using a remote control (this keeps the camera from shaking and creates a much nicer video), press record. The student then reads the first line of the poem into the camera microphone.

- When the first line has been read, press pause.

- Follow the same procedure to record each different picture in order to coincide with the poem.

- Always use the same picture for the "I Am" line of the poem (a school photo of the student works well).

"I AM" POEM

1st Stanza

I am_____ (two special characteristics you have)

I wonder _____ (something you are actually curious about)

I hear _____ (an imaginary sound)

I see_____ (an imaginary sight)

I want _____ (an actual desire)

I am_____ (the first line of the poem repeated)

2nd Stanza

I pretend_____ (something you actually pretend to do)

I feel _____ (a feeling about something imaginary)

I touch _____ (an imaginary touch)

I worry _____ (something that actually worries you)

I cry _____ (something that makes you sad)

I am_____ (the first line of the poem repeated)

3rd Stanza

I understand _____ (something you know to be true)

I say _____ (something you believe in)

I dream_____ (something you actually dream about)

I try_____ (something you make an effort about)

I hope _____ (something you actually hope for)

I am_____ (the first line of the poem repeated)

VIDEO STORIES

Video is a very good way to motivate children to read and write effectively. In this project, students turn their stories into movies.

Grade Level: three to five

Duration: 60 minutes of recording time

Materials:

writing paper, pencil, crayons or markers, white paper (8½" x 11" (22 cm x 28 cm) or larger) , video camera, video remote control, tripod, video tape

Before the Video Process:

- Groups of students write a well developed short story.

- The students make a storyboard which sequences the main events in the story and includes a script for each scene.

- Students draw and color several scenes for their stories. Tell students to make the pictures very dark (taping tends to lighten the color) and focus the drawing in the center of the paper (taping will cut out things on the edges of the paper).

- Remind students to create a title page for their stories.

- Have students practice reading the script that goes with each different scene.

During the Video Process:

- Place the title page on a flat surface (on the floor or tape to the wall). Angle the camera so that the title is in the view finder. Zoom the lens so that only the paper shows.

- Using the remote control (or being careful not to bump the camera), press record.

- Select a narrator. Have the narrator read the name of the story and the authors into the camera microphone. Press pause.

- Place the next scene in position. Adjust the camera as necessary.

- Read and record narration for that scene, then press pause.

- Repeat until all scenes and narration are recorded.

- Watch your creation on TV.

VIDEO STORYBOARD 1

Directions: Use the boxes for simple line drawings to represent the graphics screens. Use the lines below the boxes to record the sequence for the video script. Number each slide in order.

VIDEO STORYBOARD 2

Directions: Draw scenes in the bubbles. Write a script for each scene below and number each slide in order.

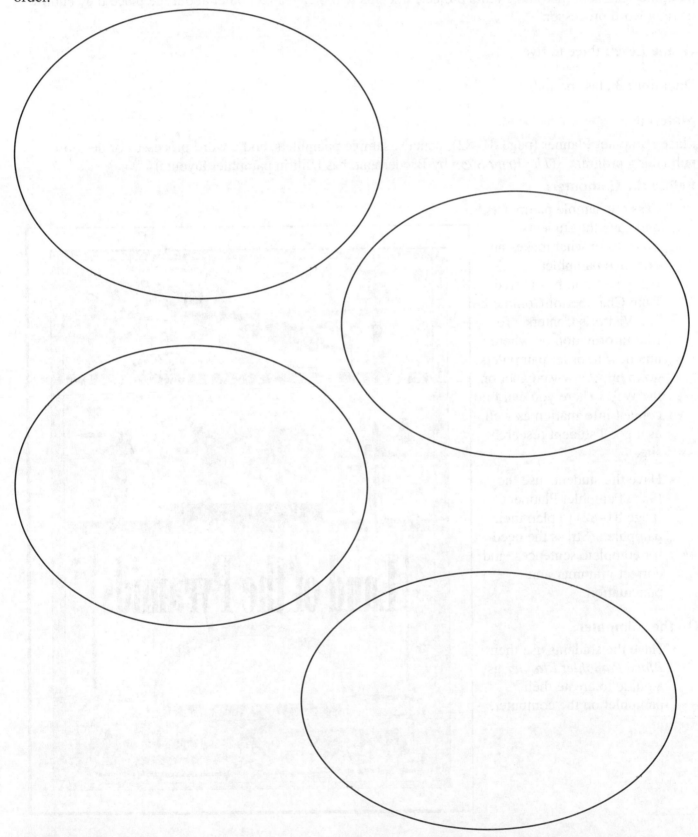

PLACE PAMPHLETS

A creative way to have students demonstrate their knowledge of a city, state, or country is to create a pamphlet that advertises it. In this project, students will create a pamphlet about the place they choose using a word processor.

Grade Level: three to five

Duration: 3 class periods

Materials:

Place Pamphlet Planner (page 81–82), pencils, sample pamphlets, and a word processor or desktop publishing program. (*The Print Shop* by Broderbund has built in pamphlet layouts)

Before the Computer:

- Pass out sample pamphlets and have the students brainstorm what makes an effective pamphlet. Pamphlets can be ordered from Chamber of Commerce and Visitor's Centers. To find information on where and how to order pamphlets, go to http://www.city.net on the Web. There you can find contact information as well as a good student research site.

- Have the students use the Place Pamphlet Planner (page 81–82) to plan their pamphlet. Stress the need for complete sentences, and correct grammar and punctuation.

On the Computer:

- Have the students use their *Place Pamphlet Planner* as a guide to create their pamphlet on the computer.

80

PLACE PAMPHLET PLANNER

Name: _____

Date: _____

Directions: Draw in a rough layout of how you want your pamplet to look. Make notes about what graphics and text you will use.

Inside Left

Inside Middle

Inside Right

PLACE PAMPHLET PLANNER

Name: _____ Date: _____

Directions: Draw in a rough layout of how you want your pamplet to look. Make notes about what graphics and text you will use.

Fold

Back

Cover

VOICE OVERS

Grade Level: three to five

Duration: 60 minutes

Materials:
VCR, videotape, camcorder with audio dub features

Procedure:

Before the Video Process:

- Record commercials, home shopping programs, news broadcasts, sporting events, cartoons, and movies using a VCR.

- Let students view the videotaped selections.

- Have students write their own stories or dialogues for the taped programs.

- Students may need to watch the taped programs over and over while writing dialogue for the programs. Encourage the students to try to match the dialogue with the subject matter.

During the Video Process:

- Replay the taped program or segment through the camcorder. Using the audio-dub option, have the students speak the dialogue they have written.

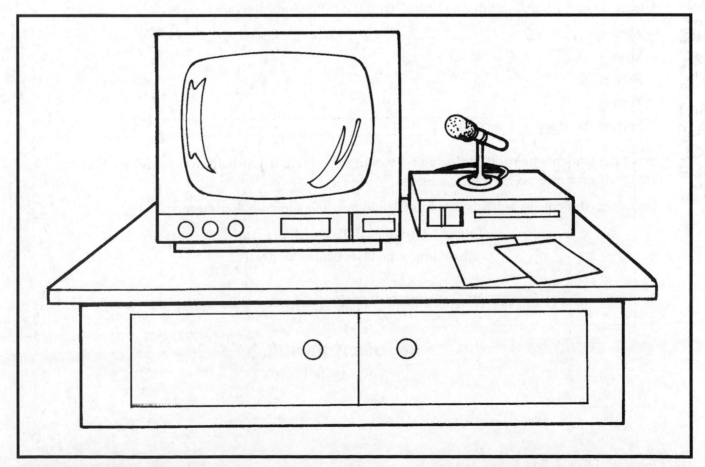

STORYTELLING

Storytelling is one of the oldest known forms of communication of events or ideas. In this project students integrate the use of the Internet and video to learn how to tell an effective story.

Grade Level: three to five

Duration: 60 minutes on the computer

Materials:

Examples of legends or folktales on the Internet

Procedure:

- To learn more about the art of storytelling and its origin, explore:

    Eldrbarry's Storytelling Page

    http://www.seanet.com/~eldrbarry/index.htm

- Look specifically in "The Art of Storytelling" section at "An Article on Storytelling."
- As a class discuss:

    What is storytelling?

    The history of storytelling.

- Create a chart titled "Telling the Story" with the following categories:

    Atmosphere

    Voice

    Expression

    Timing

    Ending the story

- Have the students help fill in the chart by brainstorming a list of helpful hints for each of the categories for effectively telling stories.
- Introduce students to legends and folktales by reading some on the Internet:

    Tales of Wonder: Folk and Fairy Tales

    http://itpubs.ucdavis.edu/richard/tales/

    or

    http://members.aol.com/storypage/jmaroon2.htm

    and

    Storycraft Web Site

    http://www.storycraft.com

STORYTELLING *(cont.)*

- Explain that many of these stories were created by storytellers, who passed them on to others orally, not in writing. Only later were they written down. Tell students that they are going to become oral storytellers themselves. They will choose a story to learn and then present the story as part of a storytelling festival.

- Divide students into storytelling teams. Give students time to do research and to choose a story on the Internet. Remind students that their stories will be performed and that they might want to choose a story that lends itself to a dramatic reading or presentation.

- The group should study the story and make a plan for how they would like to perform, or "tell," it. For example, students may want to assign different parts of the story to each group member or have one group member act out a part or play an instrument, etc. The group should know the beginning, middle, and end of their story.

- Encourage students to be creative about their presentations. Some students may want to add music and props, some may be able to incorporate costumes or rhythmic movements.

- Allow enough rehearsal time for each group. Hold the first performances in the classroom. Then discuss with students how to share the storytelling with other classes, or with family and community members.

- Videotape the presentations and make them available in the school library. You might also share the tape with a class in another community that is studying the same, or a related, theme.

RENGA CHAIN POEMS

The renga is a collective poem which became popular in Japan. Each poet contributing in the communal writing of the renga would lend his voice to the poet before him. In this project, students use video to create their renga.

Grade Level: three to five

Duration: 60 minutes

Materials:

laserdiscs, laserdisc player, VCR, video tape, camcorder or VCR with audio dub features, Renga Worksheet (Page 87)

Procedure:

Before the Video Process:

- Arrange students in groups of 4 to 5.

- Search through laserdisc footage.

- Select a frame to use as a stimulus for the poem.

- Each person in the group writes the first line of a poem on paper, expressing a thought exemplified by the picture.

- Everyone in the group passes his or her paper to the person on his or her right. That person writes the second line of the poem, keeping with the thought and mood of the first line.

- Each group member continues to pass to the right, adding to the lines of poetry until the poem is back to the person who wrote the first line.

- Each person reads his or her poem to the group. The group then decides which poem to record.

- Select music to set the mood for the poem.

During the Video Process:

- Videotape the laserdisc frame for about five minutes.

- Audio dub the voice and music over the video picture. Each student should read his or her own line of the poem while playing the music.

- Watch the finished product on television.

RENGA CHAIN POEMS *(cont.)*

RENGA WORKSHEET

Picture Chosen: Laserdisc _____   Frame Number ____

Description _____

1st Line_____

_____

2nd Line _____

_____

3rd Line _____

_____

4th Line_____

_____

5th Line_____

_____

PUBLIC SERVICE ANNOUNCEMENTS

Perfect for the culmination of a unit on current events, in this project students create public service radio or TV spots to encourage awareness of conservation or public concern issues.

Grade Level: three to five

Duration: 60 minutes

Materials:

paper, pencil, audio or audiovisual recording equipment, props and costumes as appropriate

Procedure:

- Students choose a conservation issue to write a public service announcement about. You may have an issue of local concern, or your students may be interested in a global topic such as keeping beaches clean.

- The topic of interest is researched. Students may want to look in books, search the Internet, or interview experts to find out about the subject matter.

- Samples of public service announcements on television or radio can be taped and viewed or listened to for students to use as models.

- When students are familiar with the topic, they select a spot length for their announcement. Tell students that typical radio and TV spots are usually 15, 30, 60, 90, or 120 seconds long.

- Students write a script for their media spots. Remind them to be both factual and creative.

- Students record their messages on audio or videotape.

- Investigate having your local cable TV or radio station air the student-created spots. Many cable TV stations have public access channels that can be used for free.

NEWSCASTS

This is a great activity for students to get a chance to perform. You may want to repeat this activity several times throughout the year so students get a chance to try performing different jobs.

Grade Level: three to five

Duration: varies

Materials:

paper, pencil, reference materials, video camera, tripod, large table or desk, props and costumes as appropriate

Procedure:

- Discuss news show formats. Students are particularly interested in local news, school news, sports, weather, commentary, movie reviews (this is also good for book reviews), and entertainment formats. Think of possibilities for a class newscast. You may want to make your room number part of the show. For example, room 15 could be Channel 15 News.

Newscast Ideas:

- Interview a literature character (portrayed by a fellow student)
- Newscasts based on science or social studies curriculum
- Create commercials to be presented during the newscast
- School Sports Report
- Future Teacher or Principal Interviews
- Man on the Street Reports (filmed outside of the classroom)
- Current Events Reports
- Field Trip News
- Interview an animal (have a student use a puppet to portray the animal)

NEWSCASTS *(cont.)*

Note: *Make sure to get permission from parents before videotaping students. You may want to prepare a permission slip at the beginning of the year or have it ready at Back-to-school Night. This may eliminate problems later.*

- Divide into teams. Advance preparation is crucial. Teams can be created to handle the jobs necessary for production. Cut out and distribute the discussion prompts on page 91 to help each team get started. Teams may include:

Research

These students select the subject area to be reported on and find all of the necessary information on the topic.

Scripting

This group plans and writes the scripts for the newscast.

Pre-Production

This group sets the stage for production. They are in charge of all props, costumes, backgrounds, graphics, and sound effects. Some may illustrate scenes for use in production. This group may want to set up a desk to be used as a newsdesk for the anchors. A world map placed behind the desk helps to set the scene.

Production

This is the crew in charge of camera operation. They operate all of the equipment (always use a tripod to keep the scene steady) and shoot the scenes.

Anchors

These three to six students sit in front of the camera. Set up a large table or desk where they will sit. These students read the written reports, speaking directly to the camera.

Post-Production

This group edits and makes changes if needed. This may involve adding music or voice-overs.

90

NEWSCAST/PUBLIC SERVICE ANNOUNCEMENT PLANNER

Research

What information needs to be researched? Who will be in charge of getting the information or doing interviews?

Scripting

Who will write the scripts? What information is most important to be in the script?

Pre-Production

What props, costumes, backgrounds, graphics, and sound effects will be needed? (Example: A desk to be used as a newsdesk for the anchors with a world map placed behind the desk helps to set the scene.) Who will be in charge of this?

Production

Who will be in charge of the camera operation?

Anchors

Who will be on camera?

Post Production

Who will be in charge of editing?

VOCABULARY VIDEOS

This is a fun and motivating way for students to learn new vocabulary.

Grade Level: three to five

Duration: 60 minutes recording time

Materials:

magazine pictures or laserdisc footage, video camera, tripod, video tape, dictionaries, VCR

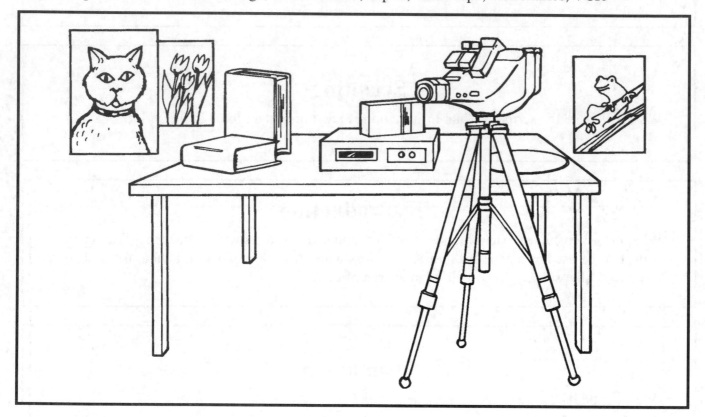

Procedure:

Before the Video Process:

- Pre-select vocabulary words to be used for this activity (this works especially well for words that are very visual such as land forms, landmarks, animal and plant names, etc.).

- Pre-test students on the vocabulary words.

- Assign each student in the class one of the vocabulary words.

- Instruct each student to find the definition of the word. You may need to review the use of dictionaries before this lesson.

- Once students are familiar with their definitions, tell them to locate a picture (from a magazine or laserdisc frame) that represents the word.

- Students should practice reading their definitions clearly several times.

- Set up the video camera on a tripod.

VOCABULARY VIDEOS *(cont.)*

During the Video Process:

- Line students up with their definitions and pictures ready.

- Using a video transfer box or taping the pictures to a wall, prepare the first picture for recording. Aim the camera lens at the picture.

- Begin recording the first picture. While the camera is running, the first student reads his or her definition. Press pause when the definition is complete.

- Repeat this procedure until all vocabulary words have been recorded.

Note: Some students get nervous while recording their voices. If minor mistakes occur, just let them go. If there is a major problem, you can stop the camera, carefully rewind to the previous vocabulary word, and start over from there. You can also audio dub over the sound at a later time if necessary.

After the Video Process:

- Have students watch and listen to the video several times (most will want to watch it over and over).

- Post test the students on the vocabulary words.

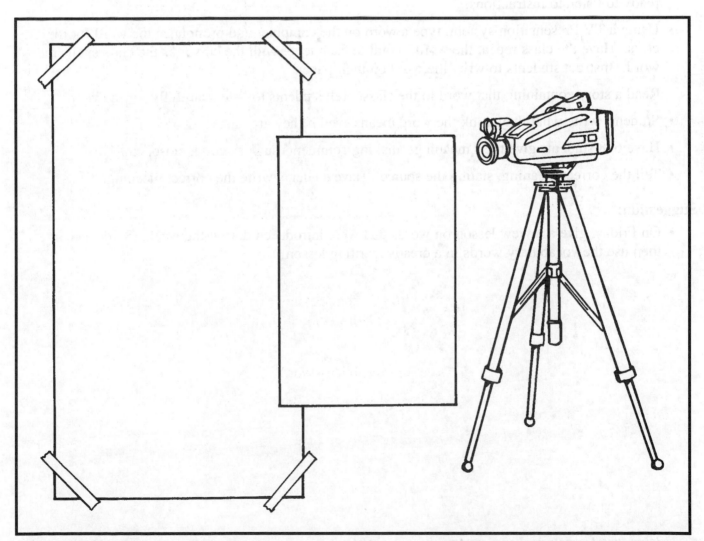

VOCABULARY BANK

This lesson will increase students' ability to write, listen, and increase their vocabulary bank. The students will find learning the meaning of words is fun as well as getting listening practice.

Grade Level: three to five

Duration: 60 minutes

Materials:

text, dictionary, TV/computer presentation system, pencil, paper

Procedure:

- Each student is given one word pertinent to the lesson. Each student looks up the meaning of his or her word. Each student writes a one-page (minimum) story including the word. The story should be so well written that the meaning is obvious through context clues. (This is homework.)

Day of lesson:

- Instruct the class to write down their names, date, and teacher's name on a piece of paper and be ready to listen to instructions.

- Using a TV Presentation system, type a word on the computer and pronounce the word for the class. Have the class repeat the word. Point to each letter with the cursor as the class spells the word. Instruct students to write the word on their paper.

- Read a story containing that word to the class. Tell students to listen carefully for the word.

- Students write what they think the word means even if they are unsure.

- Have 6–8 students give their meanings, making comments such as good, close, etc.

- Tell the correct meaning, stating the source. Have students write the correct meaning.

Suggestion:

- On Friday, give a review lesson on words that were introduced during the week. Students can then use the vocabulary words in a creative writing lesson.

PRE-WRITING LISTENING LESSON

This lesson is best suited for a lab situation. This can be used as a pre-writing activity to set the stage for a formal writing assignment on the word processor.

Grade Level: three to five

Duration: 15–30 minutes

Materials:

word processor

Procedure:

Orally present the following directions to students: Select an initial from your name and type it on your screen. Think of a three-letter word that begins with your letter and type it below your letter. Think of a four-letter word that begins with your letter and place it below the three-letter word. Continue adding words with one more letter at a time until you can think of no more. This lesson can be repeated using other letters.

MYSTERY PICTURE

In this lesson, students learn to use their paint programs while practicing their listening skills and evaluating the use of clear language. This lesson is best done in the computer lab or media center where many students have access to computers. It can be continued with directions for simple geometric design or capital letters. It is designed to encourage students to focus on the importance of clear, oral communication.

Grade Level: three to five

Duration: 60 minutes

Materials:

picture of the number 5, a paint program like *Kid Pix,* paper for printing

Procedure:

Before the Computer:

- The teacher should try the activity using his or her software in order to anticipate any difficulties.

On the Computer:

- Have the students open their paint programs on the computer. Tell them that you want them to listen to your instructions very carefully. Tell them not to ask any questions during the activity.

- Read the instructions for Activity 1 on the next page aloud to the students, pausing after each instruction. Students may not ask questions. The teacher should not make any hand gestures. Students are to simply draw their interpretation of the instructions.

- Once finished with Activity 1, ask, "What words or phrases could I have used to help you draw the picture more accurately?" Write suggestions on board. (e.g., straight, 1" long, horizontal, right end, middle, etc.)

- Thank students for their help in clarifying your language. Ask them to try again and promise them that you will use clearer language.

- Read the instructions for Activity 2 on the next page and have the students draw as they did in Activity 1.

- After finishing Activity 2, make lists of "muddy" and "clear" words/phrases on the board. (e.g., Muddy—long line, short line, shape, thing; Clear—left, right, middle, ½ inch, vertical, horizontal)

- Discuss and list situations in which clear communication is vital. Discuss the possible results of unclear communication.

MYSTERY PICTURE *(cont.)*

Activity 1 Instructions

1. Draw a short line.

2. Draw another line touching the first line you drew.

3. Put your cursor at the other end of the second line and draw half a circle.

After children are finished, print the pictures and post. Discuss the differences among the drawings on display. Ask, "What questions did you want to ask as we were doing this activity?" (e.g., How long should the line be? Should the line be horizontal, vertical or diagonal? Should the lines be straight?)

Have students follow your instructions again. This time read the following:

Activity 2 Instructions

1. Starting in the middle of your screen, draw a horizontal line about 1 inch long.

2. Place the cursor on the place where the horizontal line begins, on the left. From that point, draw a vertical line. The vertical line should be about 1 inch long.

3. Starting where the second line ends, draw a backwards "C," going down. The tips of the backwards C should be about 1 inch apart.

Have students display their second pictures. Show them a picture of the number 5. (Most pictures should be similar.) Discuss why the second set of pictures are more alike than the first. (It's easier to get your message across if you use clear, specific, language.)

MONTHLY THEME IDEAS

This section is meant to give you ideas to use for simple multimedia projects that can be completed each month. All of the ideas can be created with *HyperStudio, Kid Pix Studio,* or other multimedia presentation software.

Use the ideas on the next few pages or come up with similar projects that tie into your curriculum. Multimedia projects are a great way to get students interested in monthly theme units and holiday assignments. It seems every month is packed with special events. Why not use technology to help you fit in some of these ideas?

Divide students into small groups in the classroom or make individual assignments in the lab. Give students basic guidelines to create cards or slides on each monthly theme. Let the students use creativity in planning and designing the projects.

Put all of the slides or cards together for wonderful multimedia presentations.

For more ideas on monthly activities, point your Web browser to:

Months of the Year Site

http://www.siec.k12.in.us/~west/months.htm

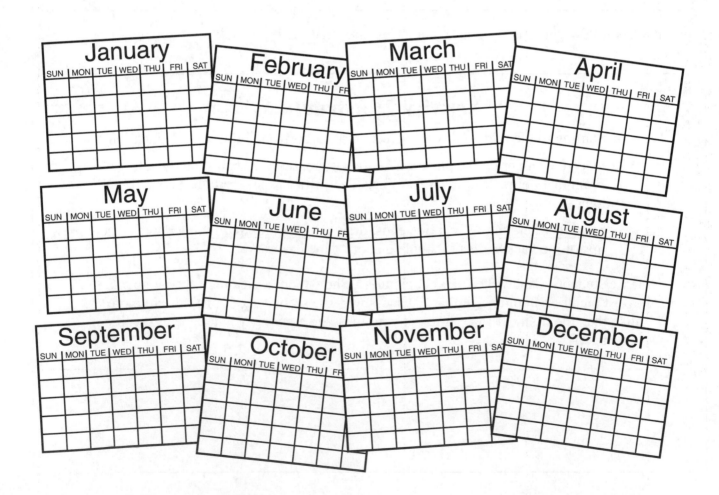

MONTHLY THEME PLANNING CALENDAR

WINTER STORIES AND SCENES

January is a good month for winter-related projects. Whether you live in an area where it snows or not, students love projects involving snow.

Ideas for Winter Projects

Students can:

- Design a snowflake using the paint tools and write a story telling about where it traveled.

- Paint a winter scene and write about it.

- Design a snowman and write a story or poem about it.

- Research deciduous trees and write about the stages they go through.

- Draw a picture and write about a winter sport.

- Tell about and illustrate their favorite winter activity.

- Research hibernation and write about an animal that hibernates.

- Make a scene showing life in Antarctica.

- Research penguins.

- Watch weather reports on television and make cards showing different kinds of weather.

- Design an igloo and tell how to build it.

- Research glaciers.

- Create a snow castle and write a fictional story about it.

SAMPLE WINTER STORIES AND SCENES

My favorite part about winter is the trees. I like when the deciduous trees lose their leaves.

My favorite winter sport is snow skiing. I like to race down big hills. I like to drink hot chocolate when I get down to the bottom of the hill!

BLACK HISTORY REPORTS

February is Black History Month. A variety of different projects can be created using this theme. To learn more about the birth of Black History Month and the events and people behind it, visit the Web site:

Black History Month: How it All Began
http://www.sfu.ca/~wwwasad/bhmhib.html

Americans Prepare to Observe Black History Month
http://www.usia.gov:80/usa/blackhis/history.htm

Famous Black Americans
http://www.webcom.com/~bright/source/blackfac.html

Biography Suggestions:

- Richard Allen
- Mary Elizabeth Boswer
- Henry Highland Garnet
- John Mercer Langston
- Mary Ann Shadd
- Sojourner Truth
- Harriet Tubman

- Alexander Crummell
- Frederick Douglass
- Martin Luther King, Jr.
- Rosa Parks
- Mary Church Terrell
- Henry McNeal Turner
- Nat Turner

For more information, check out these sites:

History of the Underground Railroad - Slavery
http://www.history.rochester.edu/class/ugrr/hor1.html

History and Geography of the Underground Railroad
http://www.nps.gov/undergroundrr/history.htm

The Faces of Science: African Americans in the Sciences
http://www.lib.lsu.edu:80/lib/chem/display/faces.html

SAMPLE BLACK HISTORY REPORTS

WOMEN IN HISTORY BIOGRAPHIES

March is Women's History Month. Students can do research on famous women and do a multimedia report telling about them.

Internet Sites About Women's History:

Social Studies School Service-Women's History Pages

http://socialstudies.com/mar/women.html

Distinguished Women of Past & Present

http://www.netsrq.com/~dbois/

Women & History

http://www.city-net.com/~lmann/women/history/index.html

Biography Ideas:

Jane Addams, Susan B. Anthony, Clara Barton, Mary McLeod Bethune, Elizabeth Blackwell, Lucy Burns, Rachel Carson, Shirley Chisholm, Dorothea Dix, Amelia Earhart, Helen Keller, Florence Nightingale, Rosa Parks, Molly Pitcher, Pocohantas, Betsy Ross, Sacajawea, Elizabeth Cady Stanton, Harriet Beecher Stowe, Harriet Tubman, Sojourner Truth, Phillis Wheatley

Reports can also be assigned by topics such as women who influence:

- art
- music
- medicine
- sports
- education
- science

- politics
- literature
- business
- architecture
- journalism

SAMPLE WOMEN IN HISTORY BIOGRAPHIES

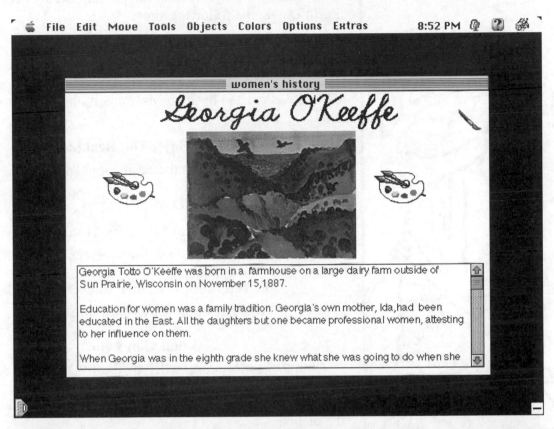

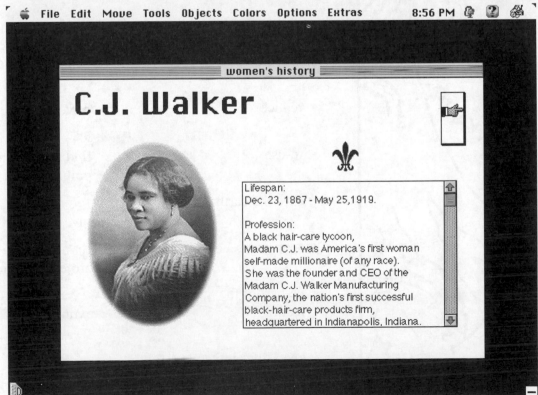

EARTH DAY MESSAGES

April 22nd is Earth Day. Students can create slides or cards with messages for protecting the planet. Students can research Earth Day at the following sites:

Earth Site

http://www.earthsite.org:80/

This site is created by John McConnell, the founder of Earth Day.

Earth Day - The Real Story

http://www.themesh.com/eday.html

Select "History of Earth Day" when you get to this site.

Earth Day: Healthy Thinking

http://www.interlog.com/~infoland/ecoland/earth2.html

The Internet Consumer Recycling Guide

http://www.best.COM/~dillon/recycle/

What Can I Do?

http://www.cam.org/~cdsl_ps/Earth_Day/i-can-do.htm

This site lists ways to contribute to the clean-up and care of the planet.

Message Ideas

- recycle
- reduce
- re-use
- save the earth
- keep our beaches clean
- be part of the green team
- keep litter in its place

- be earth friendly
- protect our planet
- find a solution for pollution
- save our coral reefs
- protect the rain forests
- extinction is forever

SAMPLE EARTH DAY MESSAGES

HAIKU POETRY

When the rain has gone
they awaken in the Spring,
pushing through the soil.

Haiku is a form of unrhymed poetry that originated in ancient Japan. This type of poetry is perfect for slide shows or stacks.

Haiku poetry usually describes things from nature or the seasons. Students can write simple, but beautiful three-lined poems on each slide or card. Paint tools and stamps can be used to illustrate the poems.

Some good Web sites to visit before starting the project are:

Haiku for People

http://home.sn.no/home/keitoy/haiku.html

and

Haiku Moon

http://www.cyberhost.net/lennartz/moon.htm

A very interesting site is called Haiku-O-Matic. This site has a Haiku Toaster that serves up haiku straight-up or scrambled. You can also submit your own haiku to this site.

Haiku-O-Matic

http://www.smalltime.com/nowhere/rhubarb/haiku.cgi

Haiku Form

Line 1 - five syllables
Line 2 - seven syllables
Line 3 - five syllables

While studying Japanese writing, you may want to discuss Japanese paper folding or origami. A good Web site for information is:

Lincoln School's Origami Links Page

http://www.mind.net/music/origami.html

Japanese-American history and cultural resources can be found at:

Seabrook Internet Media Project

http://www.well.com/user/kadani

SAMPLE HAIKU POETRY

RAINBOW HAIKU

The rain comes falling
until the sun dries it up
and makes a rainbow.

MOUNTAIN HAIKU

SNOW-CAPPED MOUNTAINS SOAR
REACHING TO THE BRIGHT BLUE SKY.
THEY ARE BEAUTIFUL.

AUTOBIOGRAPHIES

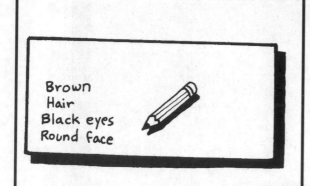

Autobiographical projects are the perfect opportunity to reflect on the entire school year. These can be very personal or more like an electronic portfolio about the school year. Students may want to take this opportunity to trace their roots and create family trees. Students can begin their research at:

Genealogy Resource Page
http://ftp.cac.psu.edu/~saw/genealogy.html

Ideas for Personal Autobiography Projects

Students can:

- Scan their current school portrait into the computer.

- Use paint tools to create a self-portrait.

- Include a slide or card with a family tree sketch.

- Scan family photos into the computer.

- Interview family members.

- Find maps of ancestral origins to include in the project.

- Record their own voices.

- Include sound files such as folk songs from the family's original country. Have students download songs at:

    http://pubweb.parc.xerox.com/digitrad

Ideas for School Electronic Portfolios

- Include the name, age, and grade level of each student.

- Scan a writing sample from each student.

- Record the students' voices.

- Students can write about their favorite school project of the year.

SAMPLE AUTOBIOGRAPHIES

"MY FAVORITE...."

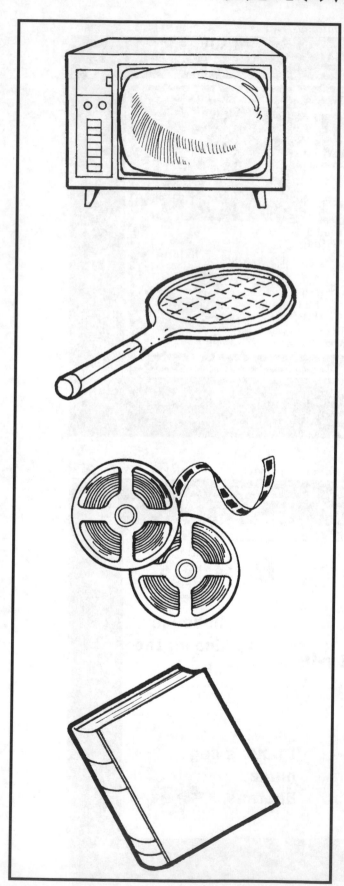

This is a simple project that students really enjoy. It gives students a chance to express their thoughts and opinions. You can assign all of the students the same topic, or you can let each student choose his or her own "favorite" about which to create a card or slide. Make sure they include a reason for their answers.

Ideas for Favorites

- food
- color
- song
- sport
- hobby
- movie
- musical group
- friend
- ice cream
- tv show
- book
- celebrity
- school subject
- activity
- teacher
- animal
- holiday
- season
- place
- vacation
- grade in school
- computer game

SAMPLE "MY FAVORITE...."

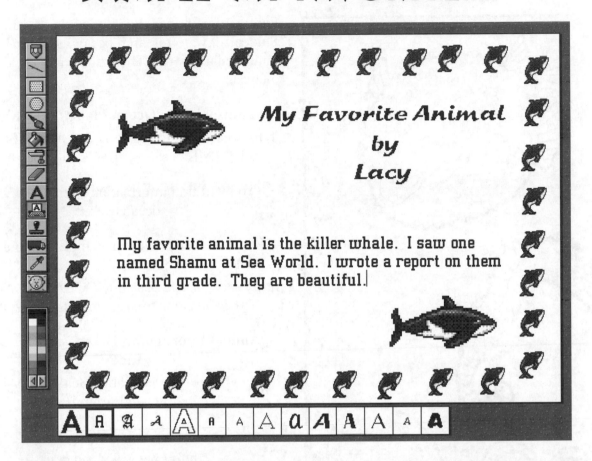

My Favorite Animal
by
Lacy

My favorite animal is the killer whale. I saw one named Shamu at Sea World. I wrote a report on them in third grade. They are beautiful.

MY FAVORITE BY VINCENT

My favorite sport is soccer.
I play for the Comets.

OCEAN LIFE REPORTS

Summertime brings thoughts of the ocean. Students love to research ocean facts and create multimedia reports. These sites may be of interest:

Smithsonian's "Ocean Planet: Fact Sheets"

http://seawifs.gsfc.nasa.gov:80/OCEAN_PLANET/HTML/oceanography_geography.html

(You will find information about the 4 major oceans here.)

Smithsonian's "Ocean Planet: Marine Life Facts"

http://seawifs.gsfc.nasa.gov/OCEAN_PLANET/HTML/education_marine_life_factsheet.html

"Animal Information Database, Ask Shamu Index"

http://www.bev.net/education/SeaWorld/ask_shamu/asindex.html

The Art of Wyland

http://www.wyland.com

(See beautiful marine art as well as a link to a kids only page.)

Woods Hole Oceanographic Institute

http://www.wh.whoi.edu/homepage/faq.html

Aquanaut

http://www.aquanaut.com
(This site has scuba pictures and links.)

Suggested Topics for Reports

puffer fish	crab	coral	otter
manta ray	plankton	oyster	lion fish
jellyfish	clown fish	sea horse	sea lion
angelfish	squid	clam	parrot fish
octopus	sea urchin	dolphin	moray eel
nudibranch	barracuda	shrimp	manatee
starfish	sea snake	whale	
anemone	shark	sea turtle	

SAMPLE OCEAN LIFE REPORTS

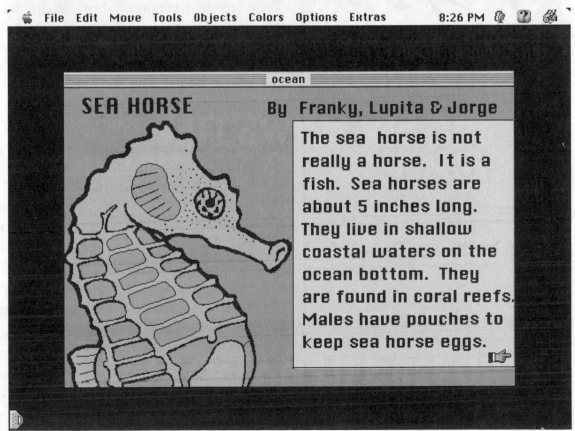

SUMMER POSTCARDS

Many students get the opportunity to travel over the summer. September is a good month to let students tell about a travel adventure they may have had. Electronic postcards are a great way to share travel experiences. When they are finished, they can be posted on a Web page or attached to an e-mail file so others can appreciate them.

Ask students to bring in postcards that they have at home. Examine the postcards, looking for similarities. You may want to come up with a postcard template as a class to simplify things. Just copy a blank template for each postcard that is to be created. It works well for each travel location to have two cards or slides. One can be for the written information about the travel location. The other can be an illustration of the travel location. A button or transition that links them together is necessary.

This assignment can also work for imaginary travel destinations or factual reports on states or countries. Students can play the role of advertising agents or tourism directors.

There are many commercial sites on the Internet that allow you to send electronic postcards. You may want to let students view some of those sites. Just do a keyword search for "postcards." This may give students some good ideas.

While the students are in a traveling mood, you might want to join in a travel buddy project. This type of project involves mailing a stuffed animal across the country or around the world. The animal is forwarded to a variety of different classrooms. Participants stay in contact through e-mail. A good example of this type of project can be found at:

Travel Buddies

http://www.owl.qut.edu.au/oz-teachernet/projects/travel-buddies/travel-buddies.html

You can also join an e-mail list to locate participants for a project like this. Contact travel-buddies@owl.qut.edu.au for more information.

SAMPLE SUMMER POSTCARDS

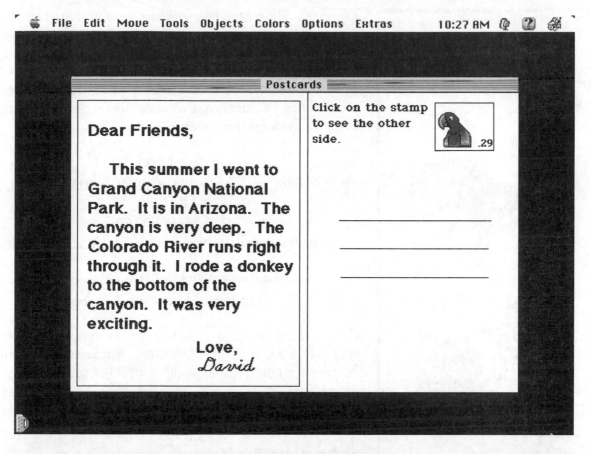

SPIDER REPORTS

October is a month when students are fascinated by things that are creepy-crawly. Assigning spider reports is a great way to get students involved in non-fiction writing.

Introduce students to a variety of spider or arachnid scientific field guides. Students can also find information about spiders at the following Internet sites:

Spiders of the World

http://www.jason.org/JASON/HTML/SPIDERS_home.html

Arachnology

http://dns.ufsia.ac.be/Arachnology/Arachnology.html

Minibeast World of Insects & Spiders

http://www.tesser.com/minibeast/

Each slide or card can include a written report about the spider, and a picture or illustration. Students who require more of a challenge may want to find laserdisc footage of their spider or create links to Internet sites with information about their spider.

Suggestions for Reports

- tarantula
- Australian funnel web spider
- orb weaver
- house spider
- garden spider
- bird eating spider
- red back spider
- purse web spider
- banana spider
- burrowing spider
- swamp spider
- Brazilian wandering spider

- net-casting spider
- black widow
- jumping spider
- water spider
- Chilean red-leg spider
- violin spider
- trap door spider
- daddy long legs
- wolf spider
- brown recluse
- crab spider

SAMPLE SPIDER REPORTS

NATIVE AMERICAN REPORTS

Native American research projects can be very exciting. There are a variety of assignments that can be created based on this topic.

You may want students to focus on one particular tribe and create cards or slides telling specific details about their clothing, food, shelter, art, music, etc.

You may want each card or slide to focus on a different tribe. Assign individuals or small groups Native American tribes to research. Let the students show what they learned about the tribe on the slide or card.

This project can also be easily tied in with Thanksgiving. Students can create scenes and stories about the first Thanksgiving or make cards and slides showing foods shared by the Native Americans and Pilgrims.

Students can search the Internet for Native American sources. Students may want to begin with:

Native Web

http://www.nativeweb.org/resource.phtml

or

Native American Internet Resources

http://falcon.jmu.edu/~ramseyil/native.htm

Students may want to visit a local museum or reservation to gather information on tribes from your region. Be sure to take along a digital camera. Ask for permission to take photographs of artifacts. They can really help to make a local history project come alive.

FAMILY HERITAGE ELECTRONIC COOKBOOK

December is usually a very busy and short month. Creating a Family Heritage Electronic Cookbook is an enjoyable but simple activity that does not take a lot of time. This assignment can also be tied in quite easily with a Christmas-Around-The-World theme.

Ask students to bring in all kinds of cookbooks. Let students browse through a variety of books before assigning the project.

Encourage students to find out about their family heritage.

A good Web site created by students about family heritage can be found at:

> http://www.mhrcc.org/pcsd/pokms/pms.html

Make an assignment to find a recipe that comes from their ancestors' country.

Students can view and download traditional recipes from around the world at:

> http://www.yahoo.com/Entertainment/Food/Cooking/Ethnic

Have the students copy the recipe for homework and bring it back to class. Students can then create cards or slides that include the name of the food, the ingredients, directions on how to make the recipe, and the country of origin. Illustrations or scanned photos can be added if desired. Recipes can be printed and made into a cookbook. Students may want to give this to their parents as a holiday present.

This may also be a good opportunity to discuss measurement and estimation in recipes. Writing recipes is a good way to incorporate language arts into a math lesson.

You may even want the students to bring samples of the food to taste in class. This makes a nice holiday party right before winter vacation.

SAMPLE FAMILY HERITAGE COOKBOOK

**Christmas Eve "Kutia"
(Poland)**

1 cup cracked wheat or bulgur
2 cups hot water
1 cup honey
2 cups water
1 teaspoon salt

1. Soak wheat in hot water for 30 minutes. Bring to a boil. Cook until tender.
2. Cook honey with remaining water for 20 minutes. Add salt. Cool and serve with wheat.

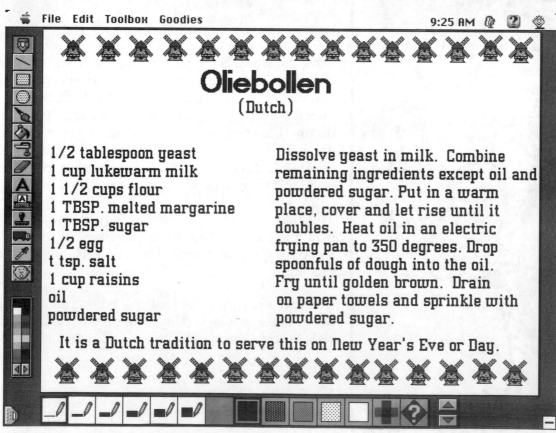

Oliebollen
(Dutch)

1/2 tablespoon yeast
1 cup lukewarm milk
1 1/2 cups flour
1 TBSP. melted margarine
1 TBSP. sugar
1/2 egg
t tsp. salt
1 cup raisins
oil
powdered sugar

Dissolve yeast in milk. Combine remaining ingredients except oil and powdered sugar. Put in a warm place, cover and let rise until it doubles. Heat oil in an electric frying pan to 350 degrees. Drop spoonfuls of dough into the oil. Fry until golden brown. Drain on paper towels and sprinkle with powdered sugar.

It is a Dutch tradition to serve this on New Year's Eve or Day.

RECORDING MULTIMEDIA PROJECTS

Hook up your computer to your VCR via a TV Presenter system. This way you can record student multimedia projects and send them home to families who do not have computers. Even students who own their own computers love to see their projects on the TV screen.

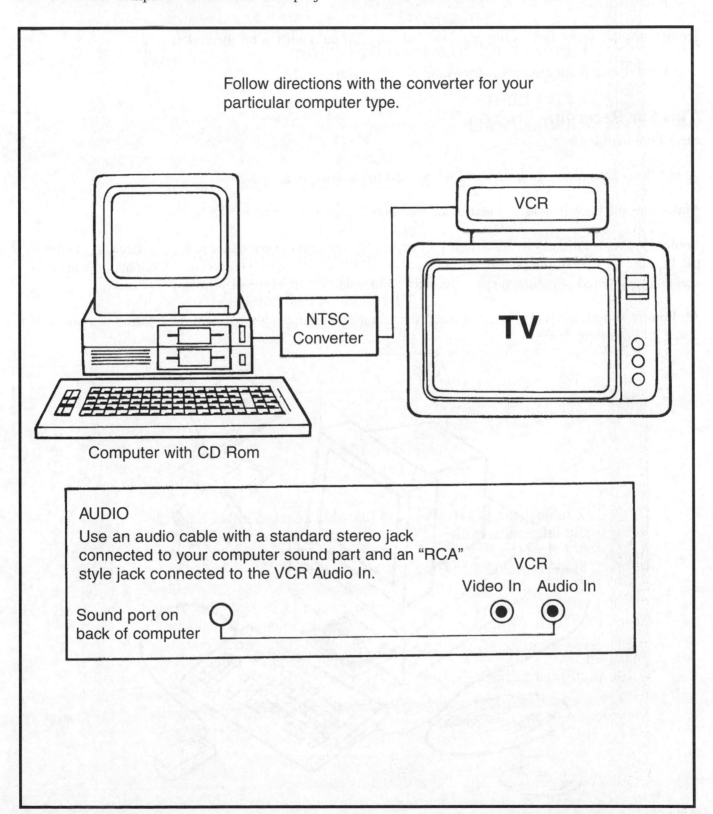

Follow directions with the converter for your particular computer type.

VCR

NTSC Converter

TV

Computer with CD Rom

AUDIO

Use an audio cable with a standard stereo jack connected to your computer sound part and an "RCA" style jack connected to the VCR Audio In.

VCR

Video In   Audio In

Sound port on back of computer

BASIC MULTIMEDIA PROJECT TIPS

Tips For Printing Projects

It is important to select a light colored or white background when printing out projects. Otherwise, you'll be spending your entire classroom budget on ink.

Remember to follow the writing process. Do not print until editing has been done.

Use black ink and let students color in the pictures with markers.

Tips For Recording Projects

Select colorful backgrounds.

Avoid fancy text fonts. Simple and easy to read fonts work best.

Make sure the background and text color are contrasting.

Some TV Presentation systems cut off part of what is seen on the computer screen. Check to see that the bottom or sides of the picture are framed on the TV screen before recording. Students may have to make adjustments on the computer screen to compensate for this type of problem.

Audio dub sound on a video camera when the narration is long. This will save an enormous amount of space on your hard drive.

KID PIX STAMP TIPS

Kid Pix stamps can be edited and altered to suit your needs. Use the following tips to improve your slide shows. Select the stamp of your choice. Then press the option or shift key at the same time to change the size. Pressing both the shift and option keys at the same time will really enlarge your stamp.

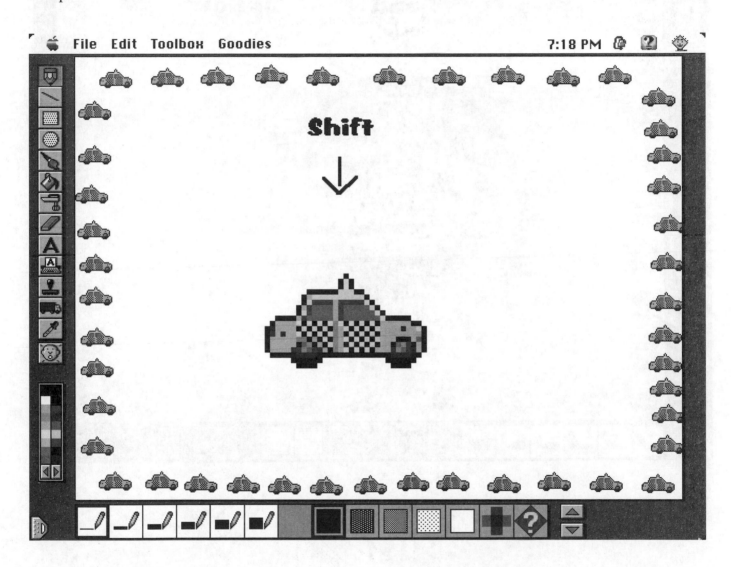

KID PIX STAMP TIPS *(cont.)*

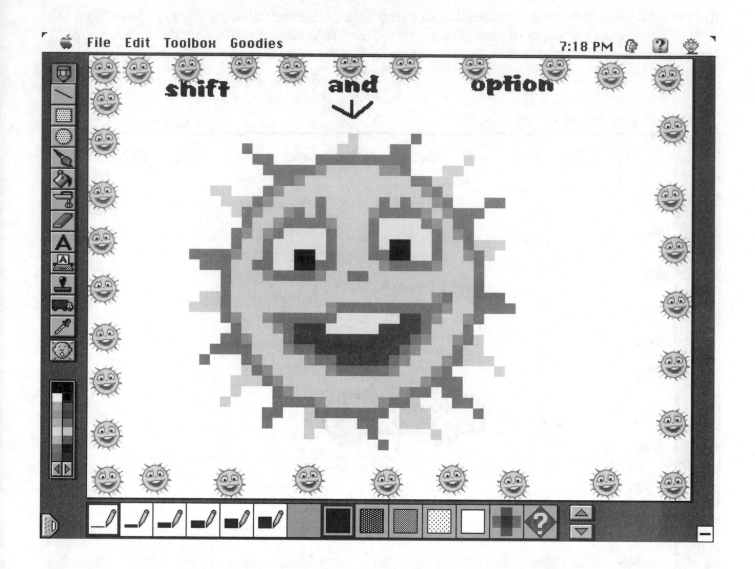

KID PIX STAMP TIPS *(cont.)*

To change the color of a stamp or edit it, double click on it. A stamp editor box will appear. Then use the tools to add or delete parts to the stamp, or change colors or direction of the stamp.

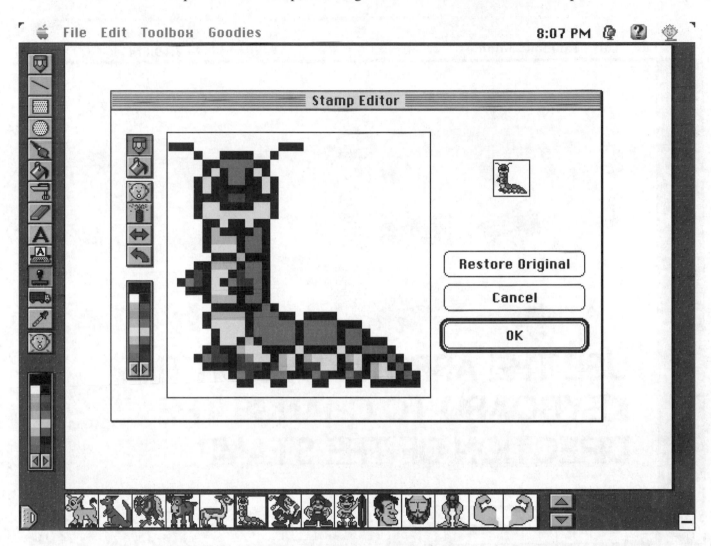

KID PIX STAMP TIPS *(cont.)*

The direction of the stamps can also be changed by simply pressing the arrow keys on the keyboard while selecting your stamp choice.

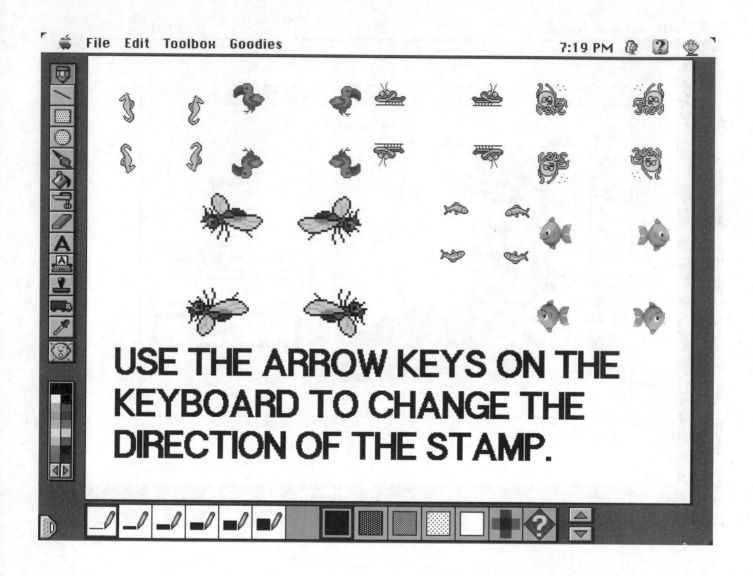

HYPERSTUDIO INTERNET LINKS TIPS

The NetPage New Button Action allows you to create a link from within a *HyperStudio* stack to a Web page on the Internet. Simply type a URL into the field that the NetPage NBA provides (such as http://www.nasa.gov, for a space related stack). When the link is activated in *HyperStudio,* Netscape will take you to the URL you specified. To use the NetPage NBA in a *HyperStudio* project, begin by adding a Button or a HyperText Link. At the Actions menu, choose New Button Actions and select NetPage NBA from the samples available. Click on "Use this NBA" and type or paste in your desired URL (you do not even have to be connected to the Internet while using this NBA).

You can also use the NetPage NBA to send e-mail. Instead of using a regular URL in the NetPage field, use the mailto: command. For example, using the URL "mailto:president@whitehouse.gov" will open Netscape and address a message to the President of the United States.

Use the NetPage NBA to give stacks a life of their own. By linking stacks to information that changes regularly, your stacks provide new information even after you have finished them.

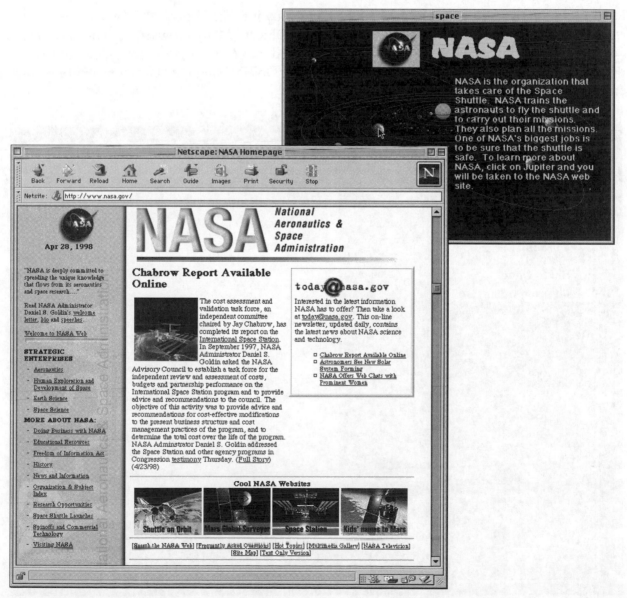

HYPERSTUDIO INTERNET LINKS TIPS *(cont.)*

The content on the Internet is becoming an increasingly important source for research. *HyperStudio* provides an easy and effective way to combine and present the various sources of media research located on the Web.

Graphics

HyperStudio supports both .GIF and .JPEG files, the most common file formats for graphics on the Internet. This means that you can use pictures and photographs you find on the Internet in your *HyperStudio* projects without using a graphics conversion program. Simply download the graphic and add it as clip art, a background, or as a graphic object.

Text

While browsing on the web you can highlight text and copy it to the clipboard. You can then open *HyperStudio* and paste this text into a *HyperStudio* Text Object. Many browsers let you save screens as "text only" or .TXT files that can also be directly imported into *HyperStudio*. Download or save the text document and then import it into a *HyperStudio* Text Object using the "Get File" button at the Text Appearance menu.

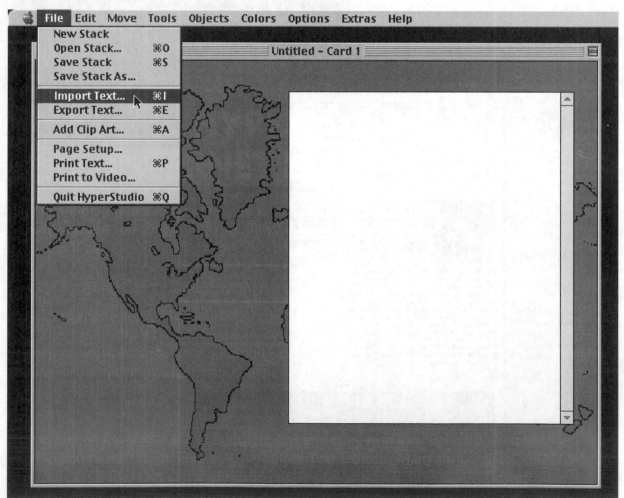

HYPERSTUDIO
INTERNET LINKS TIPS *(cont.)*

Animation

HyperStudio supports animated .GIF files. Simply download the animation from a Web site. When you add an animation in *HyperStudio* (at the Actions menu), choose your animation from a "disk file", navigate to your downloaded animated .GIF, and make your animation. (This requires *HyperStudio* 3.1 for Macintosh and 3.0 for Windows.) If your Mac does not recognize the file, you may need to open the file in a utility like .GIF Builder first.

Sounds

The most common sound file types on the Web are .AIFF and .AU. If you can move these files to your local drive, you can use them in your projects. *HyperStudio* for Macintosh supports both of these file formats. To use these files in Windows, you will need a sound conversion utility.

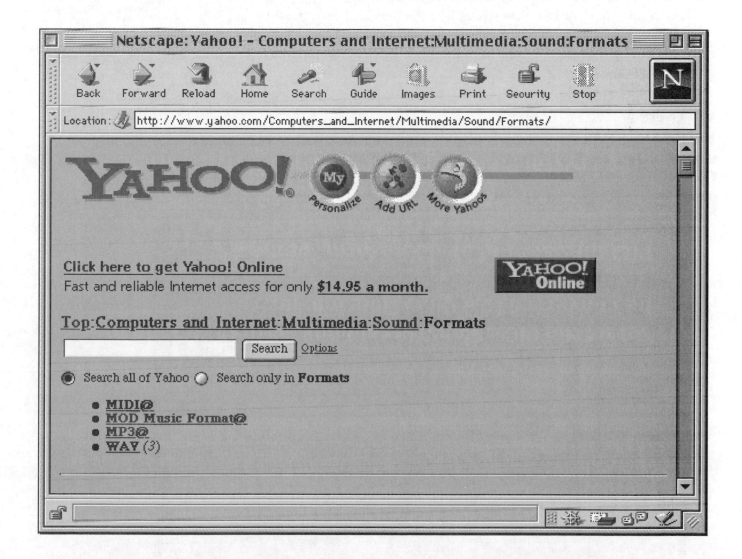

HYPERSTUDIO INTERNET LINKS TIPS *(cont.)*

For more flexibility with Internet resources, inexpensive sound, graphic, text, and animation utilities for both Macintosh and Windows can be found at:

http://www.shareware.com

A search here should locate utilities which allow you to edit files and file formats of various media.

Keep copyright and intellectual property rights in mind when working with information on the Web. Try to find sites that are copyright or license free and always document all media sources, such as artist name and URL location. *HyperStudio* provides a bibliography template under Edit, Ready Made Cards, that makes this process a natural part of any *HyperStudio* stack.

Macintosh Users

You must be using System 7.0 or later, have the Netscape program and MacTCP installed* Your Internet connection must be through an Internet Service Provider (ISP) and will not work with proprietary services like AOL, CompuServe, and Prodigy. Netscape will launch when the link is activated in *HyperStudio*. To return to the stack you can use the MacOS Application Finder or simply quit the Netscape browser.

PC Users

You must have Netscape or Internet Explorer programs installed. Your Internet connection must be through an Internet Service Provider (ISP) and will not work with proprietary services like AOH, CompuServe, and Prodigy. Netscape must be open when the link is activated in *HyperStudio*. To return to the stack type ALT+TAB to toggle back to the *HyperStudio* stack or quit your Internet browser.

HYPERSTUDIO CREATING QUICKTIME VIRTUAL REALITY MOVIES TIPS

Now it is possible to easily create your own *QuickTime* Virtual Reality (QTVR) movies right in *HyperStudio*. These movies can be added to your stacks to add fun and excitement to your projects.

Generating Still Images of Your Object

Before you create your QTVR movie, you need to capture a series of images/frames of your object. The frames can be captured with a camera or they can be rendered. The resulting images must be digital in a PICS, MooV, Scrapbook, or PICT format, and they should be saved in the form of "name.#" (e.g. object.01, object.02, etc.). Taking 36 images for each axis of the movie is optimal, but you can take as few as 8 frames and still get a great movie.

The Process

A Compression Setting dialog will appear. The default settings will work fine, but feel free to play around with quality and compression if you desire. When you are satisfied with the options, click on OK.

A dialog box will appear, allowing you to name your movie and assign a saving location. Remember, if you want to share the movie with Windows users, make sure to include the .mov file extension to the end of the movie name.

ConvertToMovie will now combine your images into a linear *QuickTime* movie.

A Conversion Options dialog will appear. If you would like to share this movie with someone using the Windows platform, check "Flatten movie" and "Single fork". Click on OK.

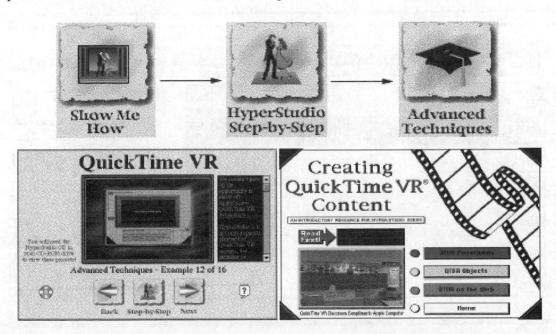

HYPERSTUDIO CREATING QUICKTIME VIRTUAL REALITY MOVIES TIPS *(cont.)*

Converting Still Images Into A Linear QuickTime Movie

Once having taken still frames, you will need to combine them into a linear QuickTime movie using a utility called ConvertToMovie. ConvertToMovie is included in the QTVR folder in the HS Utilities folder on the *HyperStudio* Resource/Preview CD.

Open the ConvertToMovie application.

ConvertToMovie will prompt you to choose the first image in your series. Navigate to the folder containing your images, choose the first image, and click on OK.

ConvertToMovie will now prompt you to choose the last image in your series. Select the last image and click on OK. The *QuickTime* VR (virtual reality) technology from Apple Computer allows you to interact with and manipulate three dimensional objects as if you were holding them. With this technology, you and your students can rotate and examine anything from everyday objects to priceless artifacts.

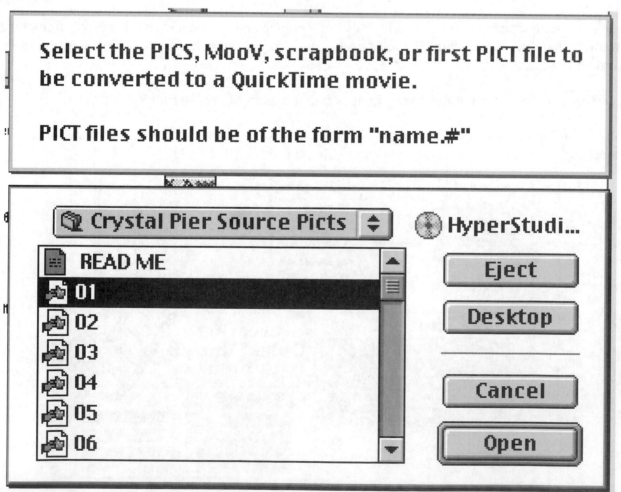

Select the PICS, MooV, scrapbook, or first PICT file to be converted to a QuickTime movie.

PICT files should be of the form "name.#"

Crystal Pier Source Picts ▼   HyperStudi...

READ ME
01
02
03
04
05
06

Eject
Desktop
Cancel
Open

PUBLISHER'S PLANNING SHEET: BOOK DRAFT

Student: _____

Book Title: _____

Illustration

Illustration

Text: _____

Text: _____

STATUS OF CLASS

Project: _____   Project Dates: _____

Student Name													

WEB SITES

Alex: A Catalog of Electronic Texts on the Internet

http://www.lib.ncsu.edu/staff/morgan/alex-index.html

Ask ERIC

http://www.askeric.org

Berkeley Digital Library SunSITE

http://sunsite.berkeley.edu/

The Book Nook

http://www.schoolnet.ca/english/arts/lit/booknook/index.html

Children's Literature Web Guide

http://www.ucalgary.ca/~drkbrown/index.html

Children's Software Revue

http://www.microweb.com/pepsite/Revue/revue.html

Classroom Connect

http://www.classroom.net

CUSeeMe Schools

http://www.gsn.org/gsn/cu/index.html

Educational News Resources

http://www.bc.edu/bc_org/avp/soe/cihe/direct2/Ed,News.html

Education World

http://www.education-world.com/

EdWeb

http://edweb.cnidr.org:90/

Electronic School Magazine

http://www.access.digex.net/~nsbamags/e-school.html

E-mail Classroom Exchange

http://www.iglou.com/xchange/ece/

The E-Mail Key Pal Connection

http://www.comenius.com/keypal/index.html

Franklin Institute Educational Hotspots

http://sln.fi.edu/tfi/jump.html

WEB SITES *(cont.)*

From Now On: The Educational Technology Journal
http://www.pacificrim.net/~mckenzie/

GAMEKIDS
http://www.gamekids.com

Global Schoolhouse
http://www.gsn.org/indexhi.html

Global SchoolNet Foundation
http://www.gsn.org/

Haiku for People
http://home.sn.no/home/keitoy/haiku.html

HyperStudio Home Page
http://www.HyperStudio.com

Indigenous Peoples' Literature Site
http://www.indians.org/welker/natlit02.htm17

International Student Newswire
http://www.vsa.cape.com/~powens/kidnews.html

Internet Resources for Technology Education
http://ed1.eng.ohio-state.edu/guide/resources.html

Library of Congress Educational Page
http://lcweb2.loc.gov/ammem/ndlpedu/

Mining the Internet
http://www.ed.uiuc.edu/Mining/overview.html

The Mythology and FolkLore Site
http://pubweb.acns.nwu.edu/~pib/mythfolk.htm

Newbery Award
http://www.psi.net/chapterone/children/index.html

PEP: Resources for Parents, Educators, and Publishers
http://www.microweb.com/pepsite

Projects for your Classroom
http://teams.lacoe.edu/documentation/projects/projects.html

WEB SITES *(cont.)*

The Reading Rainbow Home Page

http://www.pbs.org:80/readingrainbow/rr.html

Tales of Wonder: Folk and Fairy Tales

http://www.ece.ucdavis.edu/~darsie/tales.html

Teaching and Learning on the Web

http://www.mcli.dist.maricopa.edu/tl/index.html

Technological Horizons in Education

http://www.thejournal.com/

Videoconferencing for Learning

http://www.kn.pacbell.com/wired/vidconf/vidconf.html

Virtual Classroom

http://www.enmu.edu/virtual/virt.html

Web66: A K12 World Wide Web Project

http://web66.coled.umn.edu/

WebED Curriculum Links

http://badger.state.wi.us/agencies/di/www/

World Kids Net

http://worldkids.net

Writer's Corner Home Page

http://www.mv.com/Writers-Corner/Homepage.html

Writing for the World

http://www2.uic.edu/~kdorwick/world.html

TECHNOLOGY BOOKS AND RESOURCES

Books

Bryant, Mary Helen. ***Integrating Technology into the Curriculum*** (Intermediate). Teacher Created Materials, 1997.

Lifter, Marsha and Marian E. Adams. ***Integrating Technology into the Curriculum*** (Primary). Teacher Created Materials, 1997.

McClain, Timothy. ***How to Create Successful Internet Projects.*** Classroom Connect, 1997.

Sharp, Vicki F. ***HyperStudio in One Hour.*** ISTE, 1994.

Newsletters and Journals of Interest

Internet Adventures Newsletter

3104 East Camelback Road, Suite 424
Phoenix, AZ 85016-4595
602-840-6679
xplora@xplora.com

T.H.E. Journal (Technological Horizons in Education)

Go to this Web site for a free subscription:
http://www.thejournal.com/theinfo/sub.html

OnlineClass Newsletter

For subscription information go to:
http://www.onlineclass.com
or
http://www.usinternnet.com/onlineclass
or e-mail them at:
tbt@onlineclass.com

SOFTWARE RESOURCES

Broderbund   ***Kid Pix Studio***
P.O. Box 6125
Novato, CA 94948-6125
800-474-8840

Claris Corporation   ***ClarisWorks***
5201 Patrick Henry Drive
Santa Clara, CA 95052

Edmark   ***Imagination Express***
P.O. Box 3218
Redmond, WA 98073-3218
800-426-0856

The Learning Company   ***The Writing Center***
6493 Kaiser Drive
Fremont, CA 94555
800-852-2255

Roger Wagner Publishing, Inc.   ***HyperStudio***
1050 Pioneer Way, Suite P
El Cajon, CA 92020
800-421-6526
http://www. HyperStudio.com

GLOSSARY

Audio Dub: A term to describe when the original sound on a video recording is erased and new audio sounds are recorded over the video.

B

Baud (baud rate): The speed a modem can send information.

Button: An electronic item on a computer screen that is "pushed" in order for an action to happen.

C

Clip Art: Artwork that is electronically cut or copied and pasted into other documents.

Cyberspace: The virtual realm where online communication occurs.

D

Desktop Publishing: The process of creating printed documents that look professionally produced.

Download: To receive information from another computer to yours through the modem. Or you may take a copy of a document from a disk and download it onto your computer.

E

Electronic Mail (e-mail): The transfer of messages between users of on-line network systems.

G

Graphic: An electronic picture.

Home Page: Also referred to as "Main Page" or "Front Page." A home page for a Web site is like the foyer of a house or the cover of a magazine. It is the first thing seen and the place from which to enter a site. It can link to many other documents or pages.

GLOSSARY *(cont.)*

Hypermedia: A computer environment in which multiple linkages enable users to move directly from one segment of audio, video, graphic, or textual data to another.

HyperText Markup Language (HTML): A coding used to write and format documents for use on the Web.

I

Interactive Multimedia: Various types of multimedia information are presented interactively by a computer in response to user input. The user's response choices direct the computer's presentation.

Internet: The interconnected global network of computers that uses the same set of software protocols.

Internet Relay Chat (IRC): Exchanging text messages with others while simultaneously connected to the Internet.

L

Laserdisc: A disc that holds visual images. Information can be accessed by remote control or by bar code.

M

Modem: A device used to connect a computer through a telephone system to another computer.

Multimedia: The delivery of information using two or more formats, including text, graphics, audio, still images, music, animation, and motion video.

O

Online: Connected to a network or via a network.

P

Paint program: Software that provides electronic versions of paintbrushes, paint cans, pencils, erasers, etc., in order to create illustrations.

GLOSSARY *(cont.)*

Q

QuickTime: A software product designed to run movies on the computer.

S

Scanner: A device that optically reads text, graphics, and photos and transfers them in digital form to a computer.

Stack: A group of cards (screens of information) in a hypermedia program.

T

Telecommunications: Communicating with other people through the computer using communication software and modems.

U

Uniform Resource Locator (URL): A logical address that identifies a resource on the Internet.

V

Video Transfer Box: A device that allows you to easily transfer prints, slides, and movies to video tape.

Virtual Reality: A simulated environment which appears to be real through the computer.

Voice Over: A term to describe a video shot in which a voice, recorded after the taping of the picture, is heard narrating what is happening on the screen.

W

Word Processor: Software that allows you to type documents.

World Wide Web (WWW): A hypertext-based system for finding and accessing Internet resources.

Z

Zoom: A video term that describes when the camera lens moves from a long shot to a close-up or vice versa.